LEAD YOUR OWN EVOLUTION FROM WITHIN

THE NO-NONSENSE GUIDE TO PERSONAL AND PROFESSIONAL TRANSFORMATION

CATHERINE PLANO, PH.D.

About the Author

Catherine Plano PhD an internationally acclaimed Entrepreneur and Fortune 500 Mentor, Transformational Mindset Coach and International Keynote Speaker who has dedicated her entire life to helping others transform their own lives and business into greatness.

Catherine possesses the knowledge and resources necessary to make a long-lasting difference in hundreds of thousands of lives to come. With over two decades worth of experience in brain-based leadership and behavioural neurolinguistics – the neural mechanism in the human brain – Catherine helps leaders build stronger and more effective teams. She has accumulated over 30 years of exploring, researching and teaching metaphysics and has received notable certifications issued by prominent organisations from all over the world.

Catherine believes that the more people we help tap into their potential power, the more the population will become awake to a consciousness shift towards the global mindset for the betterment of all humankind.

Copyright © 2022 by Catherine Plano

Original Publication 2016
Revised Publication 2022

Lead Your Own Evolution from Within
The no-nonsense guide to personal and professional transformation

Cover and Design: Andoni Salvador

All rights reserved. No part of this publication may be reproduced, distributed, or transmitted in any form or by any means, including photocopying, recording, or other electronic or mechanical methods, without the prior written permission of the publisher, except in the case of brief quotations embodied in critical reviews and certain other non-commercial uses permitted by copyright law.

Although the author and publisher have made every effort to ensure that the information in this book was correct at press time, the author and publisher do not assume and hereby disclaim any liability to any party for any loss, damage, or disruption caused by errors or omissions, whether such errors or omissions result from negligence, accident, or any other cause.

Adherence to all applicable laws and regulations, including international, federal, state, and local governing professional licensing, business practices, advertising, and all other aspects of doing business in the US, Canada or any other jurisdiction is the sole responsibility of the reader and consumer.

Neither the author nor the publisher assumes any responsibility or liability whatsoever on behalf of the consumer or reader of this material. Any perceived slight of any individual or organisation is purely unintentional.

The resources in this book are provided for informational purposes only and should not be used to replace the specialised training and professional judgment of a health care or mental health care professional.

Neither the author nor the publisher can be held responsible for the use of the information provided within this book. Please always consult a trained professional before making any decision regarding the treatment of yourself or others.

For more information, email support@catherineplano.com.au

ISBN: 978-0-6454161-0-7 (Paperback)

ISBN: 978-0-6454161-1-4 (eBook)

TABLE OF CONTENTS

Introduction	ix
1. Change Your Mind; Change Your Life	1
2. Do You Shine or Do You Hide?	19
3. The Power of Love and Forgiveness	33
4. Hijacking Your Negative Beliefs	49
5. Breaking Down Fear	65
6. Creating the Right Mindset for Change	81
7. Unleash Your Inner Courage	95
8. Universal Laws of Harmony	111
9. Finding Your Passion and Purpose	123
10. Communication is like Oxygen	137
11. Rapport is like a Dance	157
12. Accountability Breeds Responsibility	169
13. Challenge Your Assumptions	181
14. Reprogram Your Unconscious Drivers	193
15. Create Your Own Identity	221
16. Manifesting Abundance	245
17. Your Journey of Transformation	267

DEDICATION

To Jordan, Andoni, Seth, Frankie and Kalani,
who inspire, encourage and motivate me every day.
Thank you for your support and love.
Mwah x

INTRODUCTION
HOW AND WHY THIS BOOK CAME TO BE

Lead Your Own Evolution from Within is a book about being comfortable in your own skin, knowing your *'self'* and understanding who you *truly* are.

Many of us want this state of *being*. But we're all too busy to achieve it. We live in a fast-paced world that's only getting faster. Time and time again, studies have shown that we are working longer hours at the expense of our personal goals, our relationships and our rest.

In Australia, work/life balance is deteriorating for 4 in every 10 people. We're not alone. According to a national survey conducted in 2014, the Brits want to work less, and would take a pay cut to do so. The French, who were internationally applauded for introducing the 35-hour working week in the year 2000, are now debating its merits because few people are actually sticking to it.

There's no doubt we have a global problem. Long work hours are associated with a greater risk of heart disease, stroke and diabetes. Lack of sleep also has been linked to everything from obesity to premature mortality. Constant pressure is causing high rates of anxiety and depression, not just amongst adults, but within our children too.

'I'm busy,' has become a universal catch phrase, and people can barely go without their electronic devices for 5 minutes, let alone find the time required to practise daily mindfulness – or take the time to pause and *really feel* the connection between the heart and mind.

We all need to work. But the problem is this: If we don't take time to slow down and reflect, then how can we possibly come to know our deepest desires? How can we possibly understand what makes us happy or unhappy? How can we get in touch with our passions, emotions, enthusiasm and spirit? How can we hope to be the very best version of ourselves that we can be?

Working to pay the bills, having a fulfilling career, raising families – these are all admirable occupations, but as human beings, we must also find time for play and for reflection, for balance, self-care and inner peace.

LEAD YOUR OWN EVOLUTION FROM WITHIN

This book is about finding our own individual connection – between the heart and mind. It is about unveiling ourselves, peeling back the layers and taking ownership of all that we hope and fear. It is about getting rid of those old limiting beliefs and bad habits that stop us from getting what we really want in our lives. This book is not a panacea. However, it is intended as a step-by-step guide to help you to better understand yourself and connect your thoughts with your deepest desires.

Knowing our own limitations, working to resolve them and striving to be the best we can be are all part of lifelong journey. It's difficult at times, but it is also rewarding in ways we could never imagine, until we start to see the power of the heart and mind working in tandem.

This book is about learning to let go of what you can't control and how to redefine personal responsibilities and personal boundaries. It provides tools and insights to align the head and the heart to create the kind of life you desire; a life where you can thrive, rather than merely exist. Its basic premise is that we can change anything in our lives, no matter how big or small, if we start to consciously think, act and behave and make decisions.

The purpose of *Lead Your Own Evolution from Within* is to inspire, encourage, assist and enable transformation – not superficial change, but deep, lasting, life-enhancing personal re-shaping that enables you to unleash your infinite potential and be the best version of yourself that you can be.

How best to use this book?

I would encourage you to delve deep into each chapter and use your journal to self-reflect and to embed the learnings so to create the transformation you desire and deserve. If you want to transform into the new you, I insist that you go through one chapter each week, just one at a time, step-by-step, to go through the unveiling, the true essence of who you are.

Enjoy the journey.

With love and blessings,

Catherine Plano

Mwah x

CHAPTER 1
CHANGE YOUR MIND; CHANGE YOUR LIFE

'Change your thinking and you will change your life.'

THE BRAIN HAS ONE MAIN PURPOSE: TO KEEP US ALIVE.

The brain is our most powerful tool for survival. On any given day, it can process up to 65,000 thoughts.

The problem is that, for the most part, these thoughts aren't particularly productive: We're often dwelling in the past or projecting the future, obsessing about mistakes we might have made, battling guilt, planning ahead or worrying. Sometimes we drift into fantasy or fiction. But the alarming truth is that a lot of the times our thoughts are negative.

Even with the scales tipped heavily towards *negative and unproductive thoughts*, most of us get through the day, the week, the year. We survive.

But imagine, just for a moment, the sheer *possibility* of our individual potential, if we could turn things around in our heads to make sure that most of our thoughts were positive.

The impact of severe and repetitive negativity in our thought-patterns is well-documented, because these can lead to anxiety, depression and stress.

The good news is that a great deal of discussion is also being devoted to the success of brain-training therapies, such as Cognitive Behaviour Therapy, Neuro-linguistics Programming and Mental Emotional Release (MER®), in treating disorders such as the ones mentioned above. While this book is in no way intended to be a replacement for professional help and advice, it does draw upon techniques founded in Neuroscience and Neuro-linguistics, to help you to imbue a more positive frame of mind and create positive change in all areas of your life.

We have 2 centres: the *brain* and the *heart*. These 2 organs combined dictate and create our physical experience. The heart is constantly feeding the brain through its emotional signals and the brain, in turn, feeds the heart out of the vibrations created from its perceptions.

The signals of the heart are transmitted to the brain via our blood stream through coded information cells called *Neuropeptides*. The signals from our brain are transmitted to our entire body, and while this happens in a very complex way, it is suffice for our purposes to say that the brain communicates to the rest of the body via electrical impulse. That is the connection between our mind and body.

In terms of how this actually works, imagine for a moment that you are about to do a presentation in a room filled with executives. You are having doubts and negative, self-sabotaging thoughts. These create a vibration of fear throughout your entire body, which is, of course, accessed by the heart. In turn, your heart feeds your brain, and your brain sends signals to your entire body. This goes back and forth creating a cycle of *amplified fear*.

This is how we find ourselves repeating cycles. Unconsciously, our heart and brain can get caught up in these continuous patterns that play out in our day-to-day cycles, giving us the same old patterns or experiences. Because, what we think over and over again creates an internal representation – a picture in our mind that triggers a feeling. This feeling, the emotion, sends a sensation through our physiology. This is how behaviours are created – they are unconscious.

This scenario of pre-presentation misgivings would play out physiologically the same way if the thoughts were positive – creating happy thoughts and positive vibrations associated with confidence, optimism and success.

Recently, scientists at the Institute of HeartMath in the US have been exploring this concept. What they have found is that the heart emits electromagnetic fields that change according to our emotions. By measuring these, the scientists have been able to prove that positive emotions create physiological benefits, like boosting the immune system.

Guess what? Their research also proved that negative emotions can create nervous system chaos, which leads to stress and anxiety.

With this in mind, it makes perfect sense to say that if you want to change your life, then you need to change your mind! But, like most things, changing the way we think does not come easily. After all, many of us have experienced years and years of *programmed thinking* and old habits that can be difficult to break.

THE POWER OF THOUGHT

At a basic scientific level, a thought is an electrical impulse which fires up the neurons in your brain. Neurons are brain cells – *electrically excitable brain cells* – that process and transmit information via our 5 senses. These impulses can also be triggered by our senses – what we see, hear, taste, touch or smell – as well as memories of our senses.

Thoughts are often repetitive, and because of the way we're wired, the brain listens to everything we think. It hears everything we tell ourselves. When we say something to ourselves like: *'Oh, I am hopeless at meeting new people and making new friends'*, then we give the brain permission to search through its filing system – the archives – that go back to our earliest memories, thoughts and actions. It will strive to find the proof, time and time again, to back up what we are telling ourselves.

We've already discussed the fact that, more often than not, our thoughts are negative. Some research puts this figure at around 70%. What we need to be aware of is the sheer danger in letting this number get too high because when we allow our pessimistic, unproductive thoughts to fester, the part of the brain that is responsible for decision-making and creative problem-solving actually shuts down. When this happens, we can suffer a kind of mental paralysis that can lead to depression, anxiety and chronic stress. As a result, we become incapable of finding a solution for ourselves to break our negative state of mind. This can happen without us even being aware of it.

Quite simply, thoughts create our emotional state – they influence what we do and what we say. But there is a way to control our thoughts, as opposed to letting them control us.

When we let our thoughts control us, we have an infestation of RATs!

RAT: *Recurring Afflicting Thoughts.*

How do you get rid of a RAT?

You need a CAT!

CAT: *Counter Affirmative Thoughts.*

The key to controlling thoughts is AWARENESS. Being present and paying attention to our thoughts and what we feel as we think them.

Here is a simple exercise to try.

Imagine a conveyer belt sitting above your head. The conveyer belt runs 24 hours, 7 days a week, and on it are packages *(thoughts)* that continuously pass. You can choose which packages come off the conveyer belt, get unwrapped and become worthy of closer examination, or you can place the package right back on that conveyor belt to keep it moving along.

Because thoughts are repetitive, there will be some you recognise immediately! These ones you don't even need to remove (unless you really want to), just keep them shuffling right along.

Here's an example: I am driving in my car when, all of a sudden, I catch myself thinking about something from my past. The more I think about it, the more worked up I become!

When something like this happens, we all have about a 6-second window of time before feelings take over. So, quickly examine what you're thinking – if it is something you don't want to think about, then there is time to put that thought right back on the conveyer belt before it starts activating your emotions. After that, what you need to do is focus on something that makes you truly happy, and positive emotions associated with this new and different thought will be forthcoming.

Observing thoughts in this way does take practice, but like all things we learn, if we continue to practice, we get better at it – and what's more, it becomes more ingrained as a habit.

HOW WE THINK AFFECTS HOW WE FEEL.

Every thought produces a different brainwave frequency. Would you be surprised to discover that positive thoughts have higher frequencies – meaning they vibrate at a faster rate than negative thoughts?

From a scientific and metaphysical perspective, we are *beings* made up of various energy levels that are produced from our physical, mental, emotional and spiritual states.

Positive thoughts result in a higher vibration. Essentially, this means that when we are operating on a higher vibration, we feel lighter, calmer, more energetic and happier. So, there are plenty of good reasons to want to master the technique of positive thinking.

MASTER THE ART OF POSITIVE THINKING.

My pledge:

I, _____ (name), pledge to no longer allow negative thoughts or feelings that drain my energy. Instead, I will focus on all of the good that is in my life and I will speak of it, I will think of it and I will feel it with every ounce of my being. Knowing, that by doing so I will send out vibes of positive energy into the world, and I will be so ever grateful for all the wonderful things that it will attract into my life.

You might find it challenging at first, but achieving an optimistic state of mind will bring life-long rewards on all levels. Here are the steps you need to take for mastering the technique, art and craft of positive thinking:

1. Be present and aware – once you set your intention on capturing your thoughts, your unconscious mind will work with you.
2. Apply recognition – ask yourself: where does this particular thought come from? Trust the answer you receive.

3. Identify the emotions that are present with this thought.
4. Ask yourself: is this thought real or false?
5. Why is this thought repeating itself?
6. How do I behave or react to this thought?
7. What is the purpose of this thought?
8. What is the intention of this thought?
9. Who would I be or what would I do without this thought?
10. Reframe it – what's another way of looking at it?
11. What else could this thought mean?
12. Let it go – use visualisation to release the thought and the emotional response that goes with it. Tie it to a balloon and release it into the sky, or put it in a bottle and let it drift out to sea. Engaging your mind through imagination, in the process of letting go, makes it more effective.
13. Create a new thought – reprogram your brain with a new idea or theory that will replace the old negative thought with a new one.
14. Connect the feeling – what emotion can you associate with the new thought to add substance? Really, connect with that feeling and intensify it daily.
15. Practice Mindfulness – be fully present in the moment; be conscious with your new thoughts. Practice your positive thoughts daily.
16. Keep developing the habit – when negative thoughts come back, which they may initially, acknowledge them, let them go and focus on the new thought that is taking its place. In time, the dominant thought will be the one that remains. However, you must be patient – it takes 21 days to change a habit. During the process, if you revert to your old patterns then you need to start the 21 days all over again. Yes... All over again!

This table is a useful tool for helping you to capture negative thoughts and record the positive ones (which in time will replace the negative).

Negative Thought	Positive Thought

"All that we are is the result of what we have thought." - **Buddha**

It takes 21 days of repeatedly doing something new to create a new habit. This is because, in order to develop a new habit, you need to change the neural pathways in your brain. For this reason, it is recommended that you persist with this exercise daily for 21 days. If you miss a day, you need to start over.

The good news is that while the new habit takes 21 days to form, you will see rewards virtually straight away, because the *'new'* conversations you have with yourself, reshaping negatives into positives, will make you feel empowered and in control. From this point, you will be amazed at how quickly a change in thought patterns transfers into other positive changes in your life.

REFRAMING THE WAY YOU THINK

Reframing is another useful tool for changing the way we look at things to help counter negative emotions. There are 2 basic types of reframing:

1. Context Reframe

When you do a context reframe, you are providing yourself with a different setting for the same situation, but in which a person responds differently. For example, a father is having problems in his relationship with his daughter, and these problems are affecting his relationship with the rest of the family, particularly his wife. He responds to the situation by taking his daughter to a psychologist.

One possible reframing scenario might be that he accepts that his daughter has a strong sense-of-self and can stand her ground. He tells himself how proud he is that she has a high self-esteem and imagines how useful it will be when she gets older. He goes to the psychologist himself to talk through ways of communicating with her more successfully, and to learn tools which will help his relationship with her so that they don't continue to *'clash'* and he doesn't come down hard, breaking her spirit.

2. Content Reframe

In a content reframe, you're asking yourself to look at the composition of the situation and what other possible meanings there could be. For example, your boss has arrived late to your scheduled meeting, after having a long meeting with another employee. Your boss is stressed and speaks to you in an unfriendly, hurried way.

When you consider a content reframe, you might look at the situation this way: Your boss doesn't like to be late. She felt that the last meeting went on for too long, and is annoyed because much of the content of the meeting could have waited for another time. Your boss feels terrible that she is late to your meeting.

You are in control of your words and your attitude, which will influence the outcomes in your life. Reframing techniques can help you to gain greater control over what you're thinking and the way you're reacting to situations on a daily basis.

A simple question that I like to ask repeatedly is – *what else could this mean?*

Reframing	What happened?	What did you think?	What feelings and actions that took place?
Negative reaction	My partner goes out with his mates all the time.	He doesn't care about me. He doesn't love me.	Angry, upset, hurt and confused. I cut up his favourite shirt.
Positive reaction (reframed)	My partner goes out with his mates all the time.	He likes to have a drink with his mates on a Friday night. They probably talk about football all night, that's why he doesn't ask me out.	Happy, that I have some me-time. Do my nails and catch up with a girlfriend for a coffee.
Reframing	What happened?	What did you think?	What feelings and actions that took place?
Negative reaction			
Positive reaction (reframed)			

Now it's time to reframe the way you think about *you*...

IT'S NOT TOO LATE TO CHANGE THE WAY YOUR STORY ENDS.

Reframing the way you think about yourself is one of the most powerful ways that you can change your life. But in order to harness the power of your reframed thoughts, you need them to be more than simply rhetoric. You need to believe, visualise, and commit to a new way of thinking about *you*.

You also need to *stop* comparing yourself to others. You are unique. This is your journey. Be the best *you* that you can be. Just don't worry about anyone else.

Write a list of things that you would like to improve in the negative column. Think about how you can reframe the negative and turn it into a positive.

Negative	Reframe Negative	Positive

NOTHING HAPPENS WITHOUT ACTION

Maintaining a positive mindset is a critical factor for one's success, inner peace, balance and well-being. In this chapter, we explore d the essence of a positive mindset, supported by facts from neuroscience research and exercises that you can engage in. Clarity is gained over how powerful the thoughts we have really are and the impact they have on our feelings. The aim of this chapter is to gradually shift your mindset from negativity to positivity, through a practical reframing process.

When you want to effect change, you need to take small steps and be consistent.

Be kind to yourself, always. Sometimes, old habits can be awfully hard to break and if you fall back into an old unhelpful pattern, just recognise it for what it is – a small hiccup along the way. Don't be discouraged, because you're eventually going to see real progress.

> When I am facilitating, I have a deck of cards where I have about 50 different facial expressions and then 80 odd labels. I hand out one card to each participant, and ask him or her to approach the labels and pick the label that best suits or describes their card. In their groups, I ask them to swap the labels around and challenge the individual as to why they selected that label. 99.99% of the time, as soon as they switch the labels they can see that very expression in the picture.

BEWARE – THE POWER OF LABELS

> My mother used to say, *'be careful about judging a book by its cover.'*

And, as metaphors go, this was a fairly useful one to apply to everyday life because it meant *'make the effort to look deeper than what you simply see on the surface; look further than what appears to be right in front of you'*.

Did you know that, as soon as we give something a 'label', our brain immediately begins to categorise it?

In some cases, this can be really useful, especially when we're communicating, because when someone uses the description *'friendly'*, *'deceitful'*, *'tasty'* and *'harmful'*, you know what they are talking about. When we *'label'* things, situations, events, people, we give our minds a reference.

Nevertheless, it's also imperative to recognise that labelling has a downside. Labels can distort our perception, because we can fall into the trap of making generalisations and 'expecting' things to be as we label them to be.

As soon as we label something, we will start to behave in an unconscious way. In turn, this will in many instances, predetermine the outcome of the situation.

Even though we might not fully realise that we are doing so, we have preconceived a notion and our brain (given the nature of the way it works) is already starting to put other pieces together to make up the pieces of the puzzle or to plan the appropriate next steps.

However, if we are aware that our brain has a tendency to do this, we can consciously stop it from doing so.

Because the problem with labels is that they are merely empty vessels that contain assumptions. When we accept a label as real, we believe that it is real and we begin to play it out. Most of the time, we have no evidence to validate that very label at all. It is something that we have made up in our mind. The assumptions become stereotypes and stereotypes are not fair on anyone.

LABELS ARE FOR CONTAINERS, NOT PEOPLE.

People are unique, authentic, multifaceted and multidimensional. When we use labels, we put on blinders and see only a narrow view of an expansive and complicated human being.

This goes for ourselves too – what we think becomes our actions, our lives. Labels can limit us from achieving everything we desire, so we need to use them carefully.

When walking down a supermarket aisle, the first thing you notice is the label. You don't know the ingredients, the quantities or the way something looks. You're just seeing the packaging. Labels do the same to people. In the same way that the packaging of your favourite brand of potato chips becomes instantly recognisable to you, your brain will, over time, begin to become instantly familiar with the labels you've used for people, circumstances and situations.

WHY DO WE RESORT TO OR ACCEPT THE LABELLING OF OTHERS?

Well, sometimes we're lazy, and labelling takes a lot less effort than really digging deep to uncover more information.

Perhaps it is carelessness or a bad habit. Maybe we are fearful or suspicious of others, or we lack critical thinking skills.

If we have been brought up with prejudice, then these ingrained thought patterns are very hard to shift.

Some people use labels to control others.

Often, accepting 'labels' gives us common ground with other people and we feel accepted.

Once we understand why we tend to 'label', we become more conscious and aware of when we do it, and then we can work on eliminating it! This takes time, practice and patience, but when we start doing this, we can become the observer of our reality without judgment. We can remain detached from expectations and demands, we can learn to accept and embrace people for who they are. We can grow in humility.

And, ultimately, we feel happier, because people are beautiful, but they are not perfect and it is unfair to judge someone until you know their motives.

> There's a big day ahead, so you're up early to get some exercise. As you take off around the familiar streets, you're really enjoying yourself. You've got a steady pace; the rhythm of your feet is in time with the music on your iPod, you feel great! And then you slip. Regaining your balance just before you fall, you realise you've hurt yourself. Your ankle is starting to swell. You've got no choice, but to head back home, sit with your foot up, with an icepack.
>
> As you're hobbling along, you might be cursing, telling yourself how hopeless you are for tripping up. You might be feeling grateful that at

least you can walk, and nothing seems broken. You could already be thinking how funny life can be. Just when you were starting to feel a little overwhelmed, it slowed you right back down. You might already be solving, planning on how you're going to manage all of your responsibilities with a sprained foot. Or you might be a ball of stress and anxiety that, because you tripped, your day has been completely shot to pieces.

How you view this particular scenario will determine how you cope with it.

Hopeless, stressed, anxious, shot to pieces.

Versus

Grateful, can be solved, funny and serendipitous.

In other words, the *label* that we put on something is our *reality*.

THINK ABOUT SOME OF YOUR LABELS.

_____   _____

_____   _____

_____   _____

_____   _____

_____   _____

_____   _____

What are you quick to judge in yourself and others?

When you reflect on these labels that you commonly use to describe people or situations, can you see how they distort your reality? Do you have a habit of calling all bad drivers 'idiots'? What if that driver who cuts you off is rushing to pick up a sick or injured child? What if they have just come from the hospital where someone close to them died? What if they're just someone who isn't as experienced as you on the road and made a mistake?

You just don't always know other people's backgrounds and circumstances. So, wouldn't you agree that labelling them based on your own assumptions and prejudices and your own experience of life is just not fair? Can you also see that in some situations (e.g. by calling another driver an idiot), you're possibly creating unnecessary stress and negative energy in and around yourself?

Breathe. And then look at any situation with fresh eyes and try to put the labels aside.

A lot of the time, the phrase *'it is what it is'* applies to our everyday lives. But in our minds, we also have the power and the potential to change our negatives into positives – it just depends what label we want to apply.

To wrap it up and simplify it for you to understand – if you 'label' anything or anyone, that is all that you will see. Unconsciously, you will behave according to the meaning of what you see – your label. Consequently, you get those exact results.

Label —> Behaviour —> Results

The trick is: if you want to change the results, you need to reverse engineer the process. Change what you see, give it a different meaning. Let's play this one out. If you see someone and label them as an 'idiot', you unconsciously behave that way towards them – 55% of our communication is non-verbal: our body language. Therefore, before you even approach this individual, he or she is already on the defence side of things and you will reap what you sow. In other words, you will get exactly that result.

How do we change this?

Let's focus on one positive aspect of this individual. Maybe he or she is creative. If this is your point of focus, you will behave this way and – bingo! You will get that exact result.

Give it a go, and see how you can change the world around you.

CHAPTER 2
DO YOU SHINE OR DO YOU HIDE?

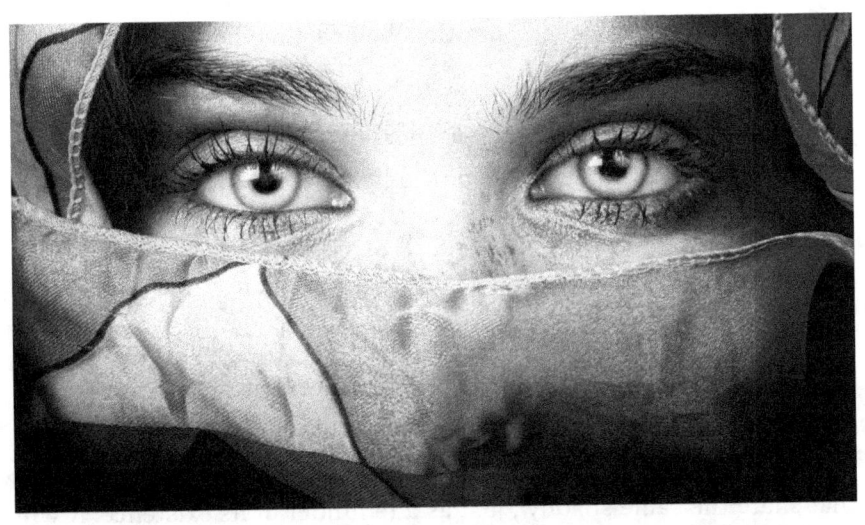

'Don't let someone dim your light simply because it is shining in their eyes.'

There's an old fable that goes something like this.

We have 2 wolves that reside within us, the white wolf and the black wolf. They are hungry and need to be fed. The wolf that is fed most often is the wolf that shines, while the other wolf, too tired and lacking in energy from no food, goes into hiding.

The black wolf is our shadow side and the white wolf is our light, our bliss.

Many of us find it so much easier to hide in our shadow side because we fear the light. Yet, the weird thing about this is that we were not born with a shadow side. All of our fears have been learned. All of the limiting beliefs that we carry around today have either been imposed upon us or created by us.

You know what? It's these limiting beliefs that hold us back from reaching our full potential.

Your shadow self is the part of you that you avoid, push away and fear. It's the part that you keep out of the light. What if, instead of doing this, you actually accepted it?

What if you embraced every single thing that you are afraid of?

The interesting part about the shadow-self is its ability to haunt us. Consistently and constantly it will hang around, it turns up when we least expect it until we accept it completely. It will impact work, health and relationships. It will keep drawing us to people and experiences that share the same shadow, just as a reminder of its existence. It will continue to haunt and taunt until we can authentically connect with it, embrace it, and make it part of ourselves – and genuinely accept that this is what makes us whole.

The shadow-self is very powerful. In fact, it holds the key to change. But once embraced, it will create a domino effect, producing changes so deep and profound that every cell in our body will be altered, and it will be possible to establish new neural pathways to the brain.

The shadow-self is here to teach. It's not the enemy; it's here to help us connect with our true selves.

We all resist dealing with our fears, pushing them further into the dark side. We all have been known to judge ourselves with comments like '*I am not good enough*',

'*I am not worthy*', '*I am afraid to fail*', '*I cannot do this*', and the list goes on...

We are all, at times, too afraid to speak the truth in case we are judged or criticised. When we do this, we repress our emotions into our shadow-self. However, over time, they build up and become emotional blocks. But the feelings we have kept buried deep down inside of us will eventually push their way to the light. When that happens, we need to deal with them.

UNDERSTANDING OUR EMOTIONS

At this moment, it's time to learn more about ourselves.

When we begin working with obstacles and learn to accept our own truth, we experience *flow*. When we are free of all emotional blocks, embracing who we truly are, we will have reached *freedom*.

But before we get to that, let's delve into our emotions a little further.

Human beings are creatures of emotion. Our emotions are supported in the Limbic System of our brain. The Limbic System regulates the type, degree and intensity of feelings.

In human beings, emotions act as indicators. They help us to gauge and identify what we are feeling, especially about situations and interactions we *do* want, as opposed to those we *do not* want. This is vital information, not just in terms of basic survival, but also in terms of how we go about our daily lives in a civilised society.

Unfortunately, most of us have been trained to undervalue the information we receive from our emotions (if, in fact, we are in touch with our emotions at all). Without being sexist about it, often men need to do more work in this area than women. Growing up, they tend to be conditioned by society to be *'strong'* and unaffected. But regardless of gender, by and large we've all been taught to *'put up with'* what's happening to us when we *'feel something'*, without truly understanding what these feelings and emotions are trying to tell us.

The good news is that this can be overcome. You can learn to use your emotions as your guiding system, if you are willing to *trust and value* the messages they provide for you. This feedback from your emotions is invaluable in helping you to evaluate the content of your thoughts. Your thoughts determine what you are attracting and creating in your life.

Your thoughts become your feelings, which become your actions.

Over time, this repeating cycle of thoughts becoming your feelings, which become your actions...equals your state of being.

What this means is that your life is a perfect reflection of your beliefs and fears. Therefore, if you want to change your life, it starts with *you*.

You are not a victim of circumstance. You have the power to be whoever you want to be. Your life starts with *you*.

If you can become aware of your emotional triggers, you can better understand *why* you do what you do. From that point, you can take action towards change.

It only takes 10 minutes a day to *self-reflect*.

Self-reflection involves asking yourself questions. And, you will receive an answer, if not immediately in the moment then definitely within the next few days. Keep a dialogue with your *'self'* open and trust what you're hearing.

MASTERING SELF-REFLECTION

Self-reflection is an incredibly powerful tool for connecting the mind and the heart. When you *self-reflect*, you need to take a few quiet moments to concentrate and be completely conscious of exactly what is going on in your life right now. You can also use this time to set an intention for what you'd like from the day ahead. Also, don't forget to acknowledge the good in your life that you're grateful for; this will help you to find a positive mental state. Remember, the good stuff is the stuff that we want to manifest!

For *self-reflection* to be meaningful, you need to examine all areas of your life, looking for patterns and situations that keep repeating themselves. Do people keep cancelling when you make arrangements? Are people unreliable? Do people love and respect you in the way that you deserve? Situations that you often find yourself in can be valuable indicators of areas of your life that you want to work with, to understand and change for the better. You don't need to be a victim. You can take charge of your life by making the changes required. Change comes from within – you can't change other people, but you can change *you*.

The rest will, quite simply, follow.

When you are *brave* enough to trust what you are feeling, and give your emotional responses as much credibility as you do your *'thinking responses'* then you begin to stand in your own truth and let your authentic self-shine. Once you trust YOU and *back yourself 100 %*, you will start to see and experience real change.

While the process is simple, it does require commitment and hard work. However, once you begin, you will understand that you may be holding on to resentment, unforgivingness, criticism or other kinds of emotional attachments that no longer serve you. These are only holding you back from greater health, wealth and happiness.

THE ART OF INTENTION

Once you have discovered what is holding you back and what changes you would like to see for yourself, you can set a daily *intention* that will be the driving force in your consciousness.

Setting an intention is like creating a map of where you wish to go – without setting an intention you are on the road with no destination.

Sit in a quiet space and become aware of your *heart,* connect with your heart space and choose your intention for the day.

Examples may be that my intention for today is to:

- focus on feeling happy
- be pro-active and not reactive – plan my day the way I want it
- see the abundance in everything I do
- forgive myself and others
- have fun and laugh
- be at peace and be calm
- practice gratitude
- be present in each and every moment and not let myself wander off into the past or the future.

You might set an *intention* that you're abundant in health. To support this intention, you focus your day on eating well, exercising and doing things that bring you both balance and harmony, filling your soul with peace.

Be as creative as you like! The power of self-reflection allows us to understand who we truly are, our divine nature or soul. Through self-reflection, we can learn from our mistakes, release attachments and reach a state of mind that is calm and relaxed.

When self-reflection is combined with setting daily intentions, it then becomes an incredibly powerful tool for change. Remember, that intentions need to be communicated with the right frame of mind, the appropriate thoughts and words, followed through by action.

Your intellect may be confused, but your emotions will never lie to you. – **Roger Ebert**

TRUST IN YOU

To make real and lasting change in our lives, we need to *believe* that we can and *trust* in ourselves.

We need to back ourselves, 100%.

Like most tasks, this is easier said than done, but not impossible. In order for us to be successful in this endeavour, we need to step out of those addictive emotional states that are holding us back. Emotions like:

- Unworthiness
- Anger
- Fear
- Shame
- Self-doubt
- Guilt

In preparation for ridding ourselves of these, it's helpful to break them down into bite-sized chunks. The reason that we do this is because we need to understand these emotional triggers, as well as *how* and *why* they impact our lives the way they do. It is only then that we can get to the root cause of all that holds us back and reverse engineer the whole process. If we don't make the necessary changes at the source, then we can only make superficial change – and this kind of change is only temporary.

Emotions – particularly those that appear to us as *'instinctive'* and which are often negative – are usually caused by triggers.

For example:

- My children are misbehaving, so I get angry and start yelling at them.
- I am stuck in peak hour traffic and I may be late for work; I begin to feel stressed.
- My doctor has ordered some blood tests. I am very nervous – I have catastrophic thoughts about my health and I can't focus on anything else.

When you tap into your emotions, you can take a look at your behaviour. There is a strong link between the way we *feel* and the way we *act*, or *react*. Often behaviour is unconscious; therefore, we are not aware of emotions until we examine ourselves very closely. Or get feedback to shed light on our blind spots.

For example, if you feel frustrated, your behaviour might be to yell and scream. As a result of this behaviour, your *guilt* might set in and then you find yourself overspending on your children or your spouse or yourself to overcome your *guilt*.

When we are in a highly emotional state, we can unconsciously magnify, jump to conclusions or blame others. In order to avoid this highly charged and over-stimulated emotional behaviour that's rash and often harmful, we need to become more conscious of our thoughts and feelings and how we communicate to ourselves.

When we take charge of the process, we can stop *'out of control'* emotions before they affect our mind. We unplug their power of distorting, deleting and generalising information to align with limiting beliefs, which results in unconscious and sometimes irrational behaviour.

WORKING WITH YOUR EMOTIONAL INDICATOR

Working with your emotions on a daily basis is one way to help regulate them – using them as a guide or roadmap to help you make the changes you want to make.

The following pages contain exercises that will help you get a better grasp on your emotions. I invite you to try them and see how your life begins to transform.

There are numerous benefits of doing this particular exercise on a daily basis:

- It will impact your well-being
- It will help you *'tune into'* your feelings
- It will help create connection to the *'self"* – aligning the heart and the mind
- It will help unblock stagnant emotional energy that could be causing pain or even disease in your body.

Once you start to move the stale energy that is blocked in your body, it is essential to pay attention to the cognitive shift that takes place. *Intention* and *Attention* while you are doing this work with yourself will have a significant effect on helping you to change bad habits and move forward in a positive direction.

So, let's give it a go!

Find a quiet place to evaluate. Go over the problem, situation or thought in your mind. Be still and listen to yourself.

HOW TO RELEASE NEGATIVE EMOTIONS

- What are you feeling? (*Trust your feelings*.)
- Where do you sit on the emotional scale? (Refer to the *Emotional Guiding Scale*.)
- Where on your body do you feel that emotion? (Place your fingers at that point and leave it there for the whole process.)
- **Why** are you feeling that emotion? (What is the **purpose** of this feeling?)

- How did that feeling get there? (Can you remember a specific time? Trust what comes up.)
- Disassociate yourself from the problem, as if you are watching a movie or the observer of your emotion.
- How can you reframe that event?
- What else could this emotion mean? (Write a list of different meanings to dilute your belief or focus point.)
- What are the learnings from that event?
- Release – visualise yourself letting it go.
- What is the new image and feeling that you would like to put in place instead?
- Now add the positive emotion!
- Fire up! Intensify your emotions. Once you are at the highest point, you can release your fingers.

Emotions control our thinking, behaviour and actions. In fact, negative emotions can be a real warning system. Because emotions affect our physical bodies, if we ignore these alarm bells, and if we ignore or suppress negative emotions, they just help negative energy to accumulate. When it piles up, it results in all kinds of physical illness.

It's imperative to our physical and emotional health that we learn to understand, decipher, embrace and manage our negative emotions. The process gives us greater insight into recognising and understanding our own moods, triggers, emotions and other drivers that can impact our relationships.

With regular practice, we can develop the ability to neutralise our state of mind and our emotions, control or redirect our disruptive impulses and moods.

Ultimately, we have the power to move *anger* to *enthusiasm* in a flash!

All it takes is a bit of time and focus.

Positive change happens in the very same moment that you make the decision to do things differently and take action, because positive and negative emotions cannot occupy space in the mind at the same time.

WHY IS MY STUFF COMING UP?

Have you ever been in a place in life where you were feeling content, peaceful and happy? Everything was running smoothly, no worries, and then, suddenly and without warning, stuff comes up...

Ding dong! Just like unwanted houseguests, do these feelings and emotions from past events barge in and out of nowhere and you find yourself drowning in a sea of negative thoughts?

There's actually a perfectly good reason for this; also, a perfectly good reason for the timing, too. The thing is, we store the emotions and thoughts we find difficult to deal with. We repress them until we are ready to let go of them and they eventually show up as a block in our neural pathways and within our nervous system.

When we are in a happy place in life, when all is going well, we are in a place of *flow*, a place of non-resistance. This is when our stuff comes up, because we are in a very good state to be able to deal with it (even if it takes us by surprise). Your unconscious mind will only let go of your stuff when you are in the right mindset and no other time. It is here to protect you during every breathing moment, all in a timely manner.

It's actually good when *'stuff'* starts to leave us. When it lingers within, it has the potential to manifest into something else inside us. Repressed emotions can sit anywhere in our physical bodies and take many forms. If they are repressed for a long time, they can cause physical illness because of the strong connection between mind and body.

> *"Our immune cells are constantly eavesdropping on our internal dialogue."* – **Deepak Chopra**

This is why it's so important to recognise when *'stuff'* starts to *'come up'*. This is an odd expression, but really it means that our repressed issues start to rise and bubble at the surface of our consciousness and we are forced to examine them.

When we accept this, dealing with the *'stuff'* and releasing what no longer suits or serves us, we are free to move forward in a new, positive direction. If you keep in mind that it's all an energy shift; getting rid of the old, negative energy makes way for new, fresh energy to give us a boost of momentum.

AVOIDING EMOTIONS

We're all good at avoiding emotions. In fact, in our society, we have often been programmed from a young age to keep them bottled in, rather than let them out where we can take a good look at what they mean. Men are taught that *'real men don't cry'*. Women are taught that crying too often or in public can be misconstrued as weakness or emotional instability.

Is it any wonder then that, generally speaking, human beings tend to be quite adept at ignoring how they feel, pretending nothing has happened, keeping themselves really busy so they don't have time to stop and think. People with repressed emotions can also have a tendency to overeat, drink to excess, take drugs or exercise compulsively.

> If you have concerns about the depth of your repressed emotions or the severity of your repeating patterns and behaviour or any addictions, then you might want to consider seeking professional help from a psychologist or counsellor.

Signs and symptoms of repressed emotions:

- Losing control of your emotions
- Not talking about your emotions
- Avoiding talking about yourself
- Pretending that things don't matter when they really do
- Feeling a knot in your stomach or tightness in your throat
- Hanging on to anger or sadness
- Problems with relationships

- No ambition or motivation
- Victim attitude
- Fatigue
- Depression without a reason
- Difficulty accepting yourself and others
- Laughing on the outside, while crying on the inside

If you recognise any of the above statements in yourself, it might be appropriate to do some self-reflection.

On the other hand, if you're comfortable giving it a try on your own, then here are some ways to release repressed emotions:

Use your *heart* and *love* for transformation. Bring your heart into focus by placing your hands over your heart. Focus internally and visualise how to transfer that fear into love, or sadness into joy, or anger into compassion. This can only be achieved with an open heart that's willing to give over to a vivid imagination, but it's highly successful in helping to shift emotion from negative to positive.

Tell your story. Talk with a stranger or a trusted friend. Sometimes just hearing yourself speak about it, out loud, helps to bring about clarity and resolution.

Disassociate yourself. Write a journal in the third person. This can help you to become detached from any emotionally charged thoughts, feelings and images.

Detach. Find a comfortable place to sit or lie down and take yourself through a mental process of detachment. Imagine that you are simply an *observer* of the interaction, situation or the other person, involved in the issue that is causing you angst. *What do you see?* How do you feel about the situation? Removing yourself in this way can help you find a perspective that is much harder to do when you are *'wallowing'* in the emotion.

Go deeper. What are you afraid of? Delve into your own mind and get to know what's causing your repressed emotion. Is it a fear of money, death, suffering, or losing someone or something?

Use visualisation. In your imagination, change the picture or the meaning you have given to your repressed emotion; this may help to release it.

Shift that energy. Meditation, yoga and massages are a great way to transmute repressed emotions out of your physical, emotional and mental body.

Conduct an 'empty chair' conversation. Sit on a chair, facing an empty chair turned towards you. Imagine that the other person is sitting in the chair opposite you. Talk out loud and express your thoughts and feelings until there is nothing more to say. Then exchange chairs and respond. This not only helps you to release your repressed emotions, it provides insight from the other perspective.

Concentrate on goals. Goals provide motivation, purpose and structure which helps to shift your focus to something productive. They provide something to attach your happiness to, and accomplishment is wonderful for boosting self-esteem.

Forgive. The power of forgiveness is extraordinary when it comes to releasing resentment. Find a way to forgive others and yourself to start on a path towards freedom.

> *"Emotions are human beings' warning systems as to what is really going on around them. Emotions are our most reliable indicators of how things are going on in our lives. Emotions help keep us on the right track by making sure that we are led by more than the mental/intellectual faculties of thought, perception, reason, memory."* **– Dr. Maurice Elias**

CHAPTER 3
THE POWER OF LOVE AND FORGIVENESS

'Love is like a lost object. If you search too hard, you won't find it. But if you just forget about it momentarily, it will show up in the most unexpected way.'

I believe that love comes in all sorts of shapes, colours and sizes; there are so many ways to describe the act of falling in love. The best love is the kind that weakens the soul, the kind of love that makes us reach out for more. Love is sweet and it is boundless, it creates lightness in the soul. Love can't be put into words and it can't be measured, but it is in every single one of us. It is our birthright to love – we are all born into this world deserving of belonging and worthy of being loved.

Now, who's to say you can't achieve that limitless love yourself? Why do so many seek love external of us? One of my teachers once said to me – *"there is nothing more dangerous than a lack of self-love"*. In class, all he made us do was to put our hand over our heart and feel the love by connecting to our heart. It was that simple. For the first time, I actually experienced *self-love*. The more you do it, the stronger the feeling. You can be in love with you. You can experience the heights of love.

Did you know that love makes you high? When you fall in love, the same neural system in your brain linked to cocaine addiction becomes active, giving you that feeling of euphoria. You can feel intense elation when you are in love.

There is research now, that tells us that the heart is our second brain and that our body responds to love and affection by releasing a hormone called 'Oxytocin'. Most of our *oxytocin* is made in the area of the brain called the hypothalamus.

Oxytocin makes us feel good when we are close to loved ones. It does this by acting through what scientists call the dopamine reward system. Dopamine is a brain chemical that plays a crucial part in how we perceive pleasure.

Oxytocin does more than make us feel good. It lowers the levels of stress hormones in the body, reducing blood pressure and improving mood. Moreover, it is linked to how we trust others.

Did you know that you could activate all of these yummy hormones just by thinking about a happy moment, or a time that you felt love? All you need to do is sit there, close your eyes and imagine; let that image get stronger and stronger until you begin to feel happiness work its way through your blood stream.

Another way to increase your levels of oxytocin is to give lots of hugs, as research tells us that lots of physical contact affects oxytocin levels.

HOW TO BRING MORE LOVE INTO YOUR LIFE?

Every day spend 5 minutes somewhere quietly and close your eyes and think back to a happy moment. Keep adding more and more emotion until you feel high; high on oxytocin.

> **Hug 3 people a day**
>
> By connecting and interacting with as many individuals daily, you can produce improved heart function and a boost in day-to-day positive emotions.

You can love someone for an eternity, but it doesn't mean that you have to be together. Sometimes people fall *'out of love'* but still care for one another. Sometimes our individual journeys take us to different places. It doesn't mean you don't love each other anymore – it's just time to move on. Love will continue.

COMPASSION IS KINDNESS

Compassion is at the heart of every little thing that we do. It is the dearest quality we possess, because basically, it means that we suffer together. A little consideration and thought for others, makes all the difference. Do you know why?

Compassion can improve your well-being, your health and even your relationships. Compassion can:

- Make you feel good and happy
- Activate the pleasure and reward part of your brain
- Reduce the risk of heart disease
- Make you resilient to stress better
- Create more positive experiences in your life
- Create stronger relationships
- Increase your satisfaction and growth in life
- Increase positive emotions like joy and contentment
- Make you less vulnerable to loneliness

As I began to love myself - By Charlie Chaplin

As I began to love myself
I freed myself of anything
That is no good for my health
- Food
- People
- Things
- Situations
And...everything that drew me down and away from myself.
I called this attitude a healthy egoism.
Today I know it is love of oneself.

Nevertheless, you have to really mean it. Unless *compassion* is connecting with something deeper within your soul, it is unsustainable.

Researchers link behavioural changes with measurable changes in brain activity, casting light on why compassionate thoughts may actually lead to compassionate actions. Studies have shown increased activity in neural networks when individuals truly understand the suffering of others and begin to feel compassion and empathy.

To be more compassionate, we need to *'meet'* people. We need to acknowledge them right here and right now for who they are. This requires getting out of our own *'selves'* and opening up to the person in front of us, asking 'who *are* you?'.

FORGIVENESS WILL SET YOU FREE

Mustering up genuine compassion for those who have wronged us can at times feel impossible. But forgiveness is the only way that you can regain your power and stop them from destroying your heart.

The power of forgiveness is in the feeling and the willingness to forgive and love.

The truth is that, most of the time people do not go around with the intention of hurting one another. We all do the best we can with the information and skills that we have at any given moment in time.

The other consideration is that many times – not always, but often – we don't have hard-core evidence of why we feel so angry with someone. It could be a made up story in your own head.

VISUALISATION FOR LOVE AND FORGIVENESS

1. Visualise in your mind's eye that the individual you are to forgive is standing in front of you. The first thing you do is say, *'I am sorry'* with feeling like you mean it. I also say, *'I know you did the best you could with the information you had at the time'*; we are all here to learn from one another.
2. Then you ask for forgiveness by asking *'please forgive me'* and wait for their response. It may be a feeling or you may even see their head nod *yes*.
3. Once they have forgiven you, say *'thank you'*. This is where you feel and show gratitude.
4. Say, *'I love you'* and, as you utter those words, feel it in your heart. Feel the love going back and forth.

5. To finish off your forgiveness process, visualise that you are cutting the etheric cord that connects the 2 of you. You can imagine scissors or anything that comes to mind.

A Buddhist prayer of forgiveness...

'If I have harmed anyone, in any way, either knowingly or unknowingly through my own confusions, I ask their forgiveness.

If anyone has harmed me, in any way, either knowingly or unknowingly through their own confusions, I forgive them.

And, if there is a situation I am not yet ready to forgive, I forgive myself for that.

For all the ways that I harm myself, negate, doubt, belittle myself, judge or be unkind to myself through my own confusions, I forgive myself.'

> *"Gratitude turns what we have into enough, and more. It turns denial into acceptance, chaos into order, confusion into clarity. It makes sense of our past, brings peace for today, and creates a vision for tomorrow."* - **Melody Beattie**

By doing this on a daily basis, you will start to feel different and you will see the results of the forgiveness process.

However, the big shift will come from focusing on you. What you have. What you can change about your mindset and your life. Gratitude can help to shift your focus – helping you to see that you are okay as you are and that you are amazing. You have everything you need right here, right now, and whatever comes your way is nothing that you can't handle.

Value what you have. The more you value what you have, the more you will have to value!

THE UNVEILING

Have you ever wondered just who is running the show in your life?

You might be surprised to find that it is your unconscious mind.

Yes, the one and only.

In fact, your unconscious mind is your greatest treasure. All that you have ever known or experienced is kept in the vast storehouse known as the unconscious mind. This great source of power that we hold in our head influences how we act, feel and how we perceive the world.

Researchers have long held the belief that we only use 10% of our brain. With new data, neuroscience tells us that the figure is more likely to be 2% to 5%.

The part of the brain that we use is the conscious part – the centre of intelligence and change – the place where we do our problem solving, planning and reasoning. It is also the part of the brain that houses willpower and creativity. Furthermore, it is the part of the brain that we must engage to create real and lasting *change*.

The remaining 95% to 98% of our brain is the unconscious part. This is the part of the mind that makes *all* of our decisions, if we are not being *present, conscious* or *mindful*.

Here, in this great labyrinth, we can get stuck in a whirlpool of repetitive patterns (old programs) that keep running over and over again, giving us the same repeating results.

However, by being aware, 2 wonderful things can happen. Firstly, we make better choices for ourselves rather than allowing everything to go along on *'auto pilot'*. Secondly, we can begin to affect change in our lives in order to be the best version of ourselves that we can possibly be.

So many of us find ourselves repeating patterns over and over and over again, whether they appear in a different year, at a different time, in a different job or in a different relationship.

Have you ever asked yourself *why*?

The reason is that we have lots of unconscious filters and programs that run outside of our awareness. Most of the time, these are old programs that serve us no purpose. They may even be sabotaging our relationships or career or day-to-day experiences. That is because our unconscious mind is running the show, and it is relying on that old box of props that include our habits, beliefs, memories, behaviours and thought patterns. Is it any wonder the script never changes?

Depending on your point of view, most people think that bad habits are smoking, biting nails or eating poorly. But the *real* bad habits are not so easy to recognise. These guys are the ones that have been running in our lives for a long time.

They might be things like:

- Perpetual lateness
- Thinking negatively or focusing on negative
- Gossiping
- Seeking attention
- Manipulating people and situations
- Procrastinating
- Resisting change
- Making rash decisions
- Being defensive
- Not finishing what you started
- Not asking for help when its needed
- Holding on to things that no longer serve you
- Spending time with people who make you unhappy.

The good news (and we'll say that often in this book) is that *change can happen*.

We can make an instant change when we become *aware* of our bad habits and choose to change them. Lasting change can be harder to master, and it takes longer, but it starts with the decision to do things differently; to make a conscious choice **NOT** to be late, to **think positively** and **look for the upside**, to **ask for and accept help** when it's offered and **to finish what we start.**

SELF-AWARENESS IS FUNDAMENTAL

The first step towards change is *self-awareness.*

When you take the time to be present, and pay attention to your *'self'*, you can see what you're focusing your time and energy on throughout each and every day. This, in turn, will create *awareness* – allowing you to figure out exactly what your bad habits are, and to recognise those moments when they come creeping into your moment-by-moment existence.

If you regularly check in with the *'self'* how are you feeling and what are you thinking? You will be less likely to run on *'auto pilot'*, and more likely to use your active, conscious brainpower to make decisions about the way you behave.

Without *self-awareness* and without being *present* or being *conscious* of our thoughts, we cannot possibly create change, and most of us have some areas of our behaviour that we would like to improve upon. After all, what is this human existence, if we are not striving to be a better version of ourselves day after day?

But our *unconscious selves* are much attached to outdated habits and beliefs because no matter how destructive or purposeless, they are what we *know and understand*. They provide a *'comfort zone'* for us to live our lives within. And, true to their very nature as part of our *'unconscious'*, they just *'happen'*.

The committed and constant effort to create internal change is not easy. It's not for everyone. Timing has a lot to do with it. Often, where you're at in your life and your fundamental reasons for inviting change can be a good indicator of how successful you will be in manufacturing change. The only guarantee is that, as they come about, these changes will be enriching and enabling. You will be able to live a life where positive experiences and worthwhile opportunities arise, because there is limited resistance to manifesting what you want and need. When resistance does arise, you will be able to recognise it and deal with it. Even if it takes some time to disappear completely, each time you examine resistance in your thoughts and emotions, and work to change it, you will diminish and reduce its impact.

Change opens up new avenues – places that can be exciting and interesting, but which can also be scary, difficult and strange. The key to remember is that at every stage you are in control. Do you want to go further along the route of new self-discovery? Or do you want to stay where you are for a while? You get to decide the changes you make, and how quickly you make them.

Is it impossible to stop thoughts?

Of course, it is.

In fact, sometimes the more you try to stop thinking about certain things, the more you can't help but think about them. For example, if I were to say to you, *'Don't think of a white polar bear'*, you will naturally think of a white polar bear.

When your thoughts are tumbling through your head – just go with it. Surrender and let them come. You know the technique for simply observing them and you can decide which ones you are going to let pass on the conveyer belt, and which ones you are going to let in for closer examination.

If you are **conscious** or present regularly, you can actively build on the positive thoughts that run through your mind and spend time manifesting them into reality. This is not some hoodoo voodoo; if you think about things that bring you joy, then you start to feel joy too.

You can trick your mind. You really can. If you want to change a bad habit, then you need to focus on changing it every day for 21 days. If you miss a single day, then you need to go back to the start because the brain needs 21 days consecutively of consistent re-programming for change to be successful.

There is research now that tells us, that it only takes us this number of days to kick out bad habits and practice new ones, making room for new neural pathways.

But remember, you need to be consistent for the entire 21 days. If you are on day 18 or on day 19 and you forget, then you have to start all over again; back to day one.

THE ESSENCE OF HABITS

A habit is a pattern of action that has been acquired over time. It has been repeated so often that it has become automatic. A habit also has unconscious behaviours attached to it – meaning that you aren't necessarily aware that you are doing it.

If you want to change a habit, it is extremely important to understand the drivers behind it. The 3 elements to identify are:

- What is the purpose of your habit?
- What is the payoff of your habit?
- What is the secondary gain? In most types of therapy, *'secondary gain'* is the term given to the reason we choose to stay *'stuck'*.

Many years ago, I worked with a lady named Jane who came to see me about wanting to break free of her resistance to change. She had severe procrastination with anything and everything she wanted to do for herself. In order to help her, I needed to understand the *purpose, payoff* and any *secondary gains* of this habit.

As Jane's story unfolded, these 3 things became very clear: Jane had an accident some years previously. Since this accident, she had been getting a lot of help from family and friends. Despite the fact that she no longer needed as much help and could live independently, she still desperately wanted the *attention* and *connection* with people. This is not an uncommon driver. It's a basic human need, but in Jane's case, she was dependent on it in an unhealthy way.

As a result of the accident, Jane had also been receiving some financial compensation. In terms of her procrastination, the <u>payoff</u> was that she could sleep in and do whatever she wanted to do because she didn't have to hold down an ordinary job. The <u>secondary gain</u> was receiving regular money for not much output, in the form of monthly payments.

At the time she came to see me, she had just started her own business, but she was afraid to give it too much of her time and attention; in case, it became successful and she would lose her monthly payments. While this stipend provided her with a sense of security, it also acted as a trap – stopping her from moving forward on her own.

By identifying these drivers, I was able to help Jane move from a place of dependence to one of independence.

In doing so, together we created a mindset for her of abundance, as well as a strong purpose of freedom. Then, for the next 21 days, every time Jane felt the need to procrastinate, instead she focused on abundance and freedom. It took her 21 days to break free of that old bad habit and when she did, she felt in *control* and *happy* that her life was not being influenced by external circumstances.

The secondary gain was that Jane was making twice the amount of money than her previous monthly payments *and* her friends and family were jumping at the chance to help her, as they were so very excited in her succeeding in her business.

Breaking a habit requires telling your brain to stop doing the old stuff and to start doing new stuff. The interesting part about this is that while you might be inclined to say, '*I am not going to do this habit any more*' (bite my nails, smoke, sabotage my relationships, and be late), it just won't work.

> "There is a part of your brain which simply doesn't understand negation." – **Sigmund Freud**

Here's why. Statements like *I am not, I will not, I will stop* or *I will quit;* will not benefit you, because the unconscious mind does not understand negative words. As a result, thinking about something that you need to give up only makes you want it even more; it makes it more attractive to you. This is *why* things become more attractive after they are forbidden.

Sigmund Freud exposed the notion that the unconscious mind does not understand negation and the fact that, rather than attempt to *'quit'* something, it is more effective to replace it with something else – a good habit – that will benefit you. With conscious daily effort, in 21 days, you can replace a bad habit with a new (good) habit.

Which brings me to this: when you want to kick a bad habit, the more you think about what you want to give up, the more you desire that exact thing. You see, the unconscious mind speaks the language of pictures, so if you say to yourself *'I want to give up cigarettes'*. What's the picture in your mind? *Cigarettes*, right! Therefore, think of what you want instead. It may be that you are drinking water instead. This also applies to thoughts like *'I don't want to be fat'* or *'I don't want to be poor'* or *'I don't want to be sick'*. Think about the image that it represents in your mind. To simplify it, just think of what you want instead. That's when you're ready to change, and here are the steps to take for replacing an old habit with a new one.

1. What will you do instead? (Describe your new habit.)

2. How committed are you to change? (From a scale from 1–10, where do you sit?)

3. Why do you want the change? (Write a list of 12 inspiring reasons to take action.)

4. Is now the right time?

_____

5. Why is this a bad habit?

_____

6. When do you do it?

_____

7. How often do you do it?

_____

8. What is holding you back from getting rid of it?

_____

9. What things stop you from breaking this habit?

_____

10. What is the driver or the motivation to change this habit?

_____

11. When did this habit start and why?

_____

12. What goes through your mind when you are doing this habit?

_____

13. What are the triggers when you do your habit?

14. What are the emotions when you do this habit? How are you feeling?

15. Write a list of the advantages and disadvantages of this habit.

16. Is your habit associated with a negative belief?

17. Identify 3 blocks that are standing in your way and 2 solutions for each one.

18. For each block, identify where the negative beliefs come from?

19. Identify a step you could take in the next day to help solve the problem.

20. Create a trigger (whether it is snapping your fingers or tapping your head, a trigger helps condition a new pattern.)

21. Always reward yourself. What will be your reward in 21 days?

The simple truth is that you will miss the magic in everyday life, if you continue to let your unconscious mind drive your decisions and control your life.

Change is easier than you think.

Success comes down to simplicity and consistency. Start small, or at the very least, break down any complex behaviour into bite-sized chunks.

As a practice run, you could do something basic like agree with yourself to set an affirmation once a day or perform 50 sit-ups. Whatever you choose, the process is simple – just make sure that you practice the new habit daily for 21 days.

CHAPTER 4
HIJACKING YOUR NEGATIVE BELIEFS

'Break free from your daily routines. Break free from your old beliefs.'

THE IMPACT OF BELIEFS

A great deal of our beliefs comes from those people who had authority of some kind during the early *imprinting phase* of our lives. This phase is usually from the time we are born right up to the ripe age of 7 years old.

At this time, other adults have a significant influence over us. This is particularly true for parents, teachers, older siblings or anyone we held with high regard.

Some beliefs come from a strong emotional experience. When this happens, the feeling creates conviction that what we were experiencing at that time was true.

TV, books, super heroes, movies and music can all have had a significant influence on us during our various periods of development as we were growing up.

Beliefs can be disempowering as much as they can be empowering. It's important to choose the right ones, because they come from your mind and your emotions; it is also possible to change them.

For example, imagine when you were a child, your parents worked really hard to pay the bills. It's possible that they would come home tired and cranky after a long, demanding day at work. They would be preoccupied with a lot to do and not much in the way of patience. They would be busy cooking dinner, preparing the following day's lunches, helping with homework and getting you organised and off to bed in the hope of maybe having a little bit of time to themselves before waking up again the next day to do it all over again!

If you were a child in this scenario, you would desperately want your parents' attention. After all, you haven't seen them all day. All you want is a glance to say, *'Darling, I know you are here, I will be with you in just one minute'*. But this is not the case, so you tug on your mother's pants, probing her with questions, *'Mum, Mum'*, only to receive a response that scares the living daylights out of you, with heightened emotions like, '*Why are you being such a pain? Why can't you just leave me alone?!*'.

If this kind of statement is repeated over and over again, what do you think happens? You start to believe you are a pain in the backside and that the best thing for you to do is to *stay away*.

The type of backlash you can expect as an adult involves limiting your beliefs, which will keep you away from close relationships. You may find yourself feeling awkward when you want to ask your partner a question or favour. You might not know how to be affectionate or how to communicate openly or you just shut yourself off.

Another example could involve a teenager. We all know what teenagers are like, right? Nothing matters in the world except *Me, Me, Me. My* hair, clothes, *my* friends, *my* Facebook page and all of the other things that interest *Me*. I want to go out and my parents say 'No' just because they feel like it. The one time I stand my ground and ask for a proper explanation, my parents' response was: '*Who do you think you are, speaking to us like that? Go to your room and not another word!*'. Ouch.

As a result of these kinds of experiences, when you are an adult you may have the disempowering belief that you are not worthy of asking for an explanation or standing your ground on any issue, regardless of how strongly you feel about it. You may find people taking advantage of you, because you do not want to rock the boat and you will go out of your way to avoid confrontation. Another outcome may be that you think you are not good enough.

It's important to realise that the process of change does not involve blaming others. The mother in our example was doing her best in the moment. She was exhausted, pressured and, as is the case with most of us when we are not in a state where we can be alert and mindful, she was thinking unconsciously. Therefore, she behaved unconsciously. She reacted, rather than responded, not necessarily realising the long-term potential for damage in her words.

Your job is to acknowledge and accept. Once you have done so, you can change the impact such experiences have had upon your behaviour, because the brain is a powerful organ. With the appropriate training and support, the brain can realign and you will be able to move forward without such limiting beliefs.

EXPLORING LIMITING BELIEFS

One very common limiting belief is the *value of money*. A lot of us seem to be conditioned by old, limiting beliefs that stem from when we were children and our parents made statements like *'money doesn't grow on trees'* or *'this is too expensive'*. Through their words and actions, our parents have created a belief that all we care about is money: it is difficult to come by, and when it does, it's hard to handle.

The outcome in this situation, of course, is that we unconsciously repel opportunities that increase our ability to earn money without really understanding why.

> ...If something in this book resonates loudly with you or brings up another similar pattern in your own life, then that's terrific. It means that you are ready to let go. Also, if you've been paying attention to what we've talked about so far, you will remember that you are in charge of change here. You are very powerful, so go for it!

Let's have a look at the statements below. Which ones do you believe?

> *Beliefs are delusions – assumptions, they are not real. Known or not known.*
>
> *Who and what we are is because of our beliefs. Our beliefs shape our reality.*
>
> *You can change your beliefs – it takes a little awareness and action to retrain your brain.*

The answer is that all of these statements are true in their own way.

As humans, we tend to think that our beliefs are based on reality. However, through the insights we've gained reading this book, we have come to understand that it is our unconscious mind that creates our reality, because it runs the show when we are not being *'present'* and *'mindful'* in our own lives. We have also come to learn that our beliefs govern our experiences. The beliefs that we hold to be true, precious and important become our identity, reflecting who we are and how we live our lives.

But, if the mind can't tell the difference between what is right or what is wrong, what is real or what is not real, then where does that leave us?

> *"If you think you can do it, or you think you can't do it. You are right."* – **Henry Ford**

Ultimately: You are in charge of your life. If you don't like something, then change it. If you can't change it, then change the way you think about it.

Take a moment right now to check in with yourself. Read the last paragraph again and gauge your reaction to the words on paper.

Are you feeling excited? Great! Then you're in a state of flow and you should go, go, go!

Are you feeling resistance? That's good too. Resistance just means that you need to tell yourself that it's okay to take the risk. All you are asking of yourself is to do things differently and that can be exciting or scary, so be kind to yourself. Nevertheless, don't be afraid to fail, because it's in the failing that you will learn some more valuable lessons about yourself.

> *"I have not failed. I've found 10,000 ways that won't work."* – **Thomas Edison**

When you are ready to start the process, let's take a look at some of your beliefs, particularly those you want to change.

> What beliefs do you see in yourself that have come from your parents?
>
> What beliefs do you see in yourself that have come from authority figures?

Take a moment now to reflect and write down what your beliefs are about.

List a statement beside each one of these beliefs and rate your beliefs from 0 to 10, zero being ridiculous and 10 being closer to the truth of your own reality.

Finally, write beside each one the consequences of these beliefs.

Belief	Statement	Consequences	Rating

The scale requires you to choose responses from your gut – really look at your deepest fears, insecurities, hopes and dreams. Afterwards, be realistic in your rating of how much of an impact it has on your life. Of course, there will be times when the effect has been debilitating (for example, shyness, or lack of self-confidence). On the other hand, when you look objectively at your life, you'll also see there were times when those beliefs were not so limiting, so aim to give yourself a balanced score.

Then, when you are ready to look closely at these beliefs and change them into new thought patterns, just follow this simple 4-step process. Ask yourself:

1. *Where does this belief come from?*
2. *What does that mean?*
3. *Why am I thinking this way?*
4. *What else could this mean?* This last question is designed to help you figure out a new way of looking at an old idea.

Probing your mind with questions creates curiosity and movement so the *'stuck'* belief that has created all of the old repeating patterns will begin to shift, allowing you to create a new thought instead. Magic, right? By doing this, you are beginning to open your mind up to new possibilities.

Don't be afraid to *challenge* your beliefs, and have some fun with the exercises!

EXPANDING BELIEFS

So many of our beliefs are deep-rooted; they make up so much of who we are and so strongly affect the way that we behave. Therefore, it is essential to spend some time getting to know yourself before moving on to the next part of the journey.

This exercise is about exploring beliefs even further. Complete the following sentences. Don't think about the response too much; write down what first comes to mind. Don't judge or analyse your response. Now give it a go!

I am always

I am never

_____

They are

_____

I can't

_____

We are

_____

I must

_____

My work

_____

My time

_____

My relationship

_____

There are

_____

My life is

_____

I love

_____

Success is

_____

Life is

_____

My family is

_____

Love is

_____

She is

_____

She can

_____

She can't

_____

My parents

He could

He is

He can't

I am

I was

They are

I can

I can't

EMPOWERING OR DISEMPOWERING?

Take a few minutes to review your responses and write a 'D' next to each belief that is disempowering and an 'E' next to each belief that is empowering.

If they are neither, just leave them blank. All the same, take time to look closely at how these beliefs are shaping your world. Analyse how they provide context to, and background for many of the situations that arise in your life. Focus particularly on those that come up again and again, and those that you find challenging.

For example, you might say, *'Intimate relationships are painful...'* or *'difficult...'* You might say this because you've been hurt, perhaps several times. Be that as it may, continuing to believe in this way is only going to give you more of what you've already been getting in this life – partners who are unfaithful, not emotionally available or not committed. Whatever you believe, your unconscious mind will give you more of it to prove to you over and over again that you're right.

However, if it is time for you to let go of this old limiting idea, then you might write, *'Intimate relationships are rewarding and fulfilling...'* You will have made the first step towards changing what you've been experiencing as a result of your beliefs. Before long, you'll begin to actually have experiences that mirror your new, positive belief about love.

LIFE RESPONDS TO DEMAND

In order to demand, you have to know what you want, because life will draw you to all of the things that are associated with your beliefs.

This is how you create your life.

We are all here to learn more about ourselves, and the world around us is a patient and persistent teacher. Life is a bit like driving a car – if you slow down a bit, enjoy the scenery, and pay attention to the signs and signals along the way, then you can enjoy the journey and it will go smoothly. But when you hurtle through in a hurry to get to the next event – that's when you can get lost, or stuck.

Most of the time, we're shown what we need to learn if we choose to. But most of us decide to walk through life with our eyes closed and we resist change. We ignore opportunities to do things differently and create different outcomes for ourselves, because being on *'autopilot'* is easier than actually doing the work required changing.

Have you ever experienced a relationship that is not working? Maybe, your partner was selfish and you chose to ignore it because it was easier or because you were afraid of the change involved in splitting up and being alone. This is not uncommon.

Perhaps your partner had an affair and you have 2 choices: to stay or go. For argument's sake, let's predict that you leave, and as time goes by you find yourself in another relationship. At the start it seems new, but as time goes on, the script starts to become eerily similar to what's happened before. Different guy. Same pattern.

To face the truth, you need to go inside of yourself and seek the answers to <u>why</u> this situation is repeating itself. Ask yourself:

- What beliefs do you need to clean out?
- What do you need to do to stop attracting selfish people?
- What are your belief systems that are blocking the good?

We are here to learn, not to be punished, not to fear, not to suffer. The universe is abundant; anything we want is there for the taking. Therefore, ask yourself, what do you want out of life? Why have you not received it?

Lessons will chase you around the world. No matter how fast or how far you run, the lesson will always prevail at another time, in another way.

WHAT YOU RESIST WILL PERSIST

Your life is a perfect reflection of your beliefs; mirror effect – like attracts like. The only option is to bring it all back to *you*. Don't blame, don't play the victim. Instead, *empower* yourself by being responsible for *all* of your actions and respect yourself for doing so, without judgement.

The fact that our outer world is a reflection of our inner world can sometimes be a difficult concept to understand. Quite simply, it means that we all hold the power within us to effect change. By focusing on our inner world and changing our thoughts and beliefs, we will eventually manifest everything we desire – the perfect job, rewarding relationships and positive outcomes with people we meet. Of course, we will also experience vast improvements within ourselves, from our self-worth and confidence to our outlook on life.

The key to success is quite simply *not* to let the outside world dominate how we feel and what we believe on the inside. We need to harness the strength of our inner world to combat the challenges we face in the outer world. By focusing inwards, we can make changes outwards.

But because everything needs balance to create harmony, we need to look at the outside world often – it works as a guide, a compass that helps us to direct our energy.

An easy, effective tool is a mirror. When something happens in your world that stirs a negative emotion – such as unhappiness, discomfort, fear, anger etc. – look at yourself in the mirror and ask yourself *'why am I creating this?'*

The Emotional Scale can be helpful in this exercise too.

Once you begin to be accountable and responsible for all of your own *actions*, you will discover how empowering it can be.

This is especially true in situations that can be emotionally charged. When we react, we tend to lose our cool. Often, we lose our ability to think intuitively and logically about the situation and we communicate poorly and make rash decisions. This diminishes our power to control the outcome of the situation in accordance with what we want/need in our lives.

By keeping cool-headed and calm, you can buy yourself time to figure it out later. The benefits are many:

- You can think over the solution and strike a compromise that keeps everybody content – this is never possible in the heat of an argument!
- You don't lose your dignity or self-respect.
- You avoid making the situation potentially worse by inflaming it with heightened emotions. Igniting it will only get in the way of a sensible outcome and also run the risk that someone will get their feelings hurt.

When someone hits a *'hot button'* within us, it's easy to get carried away with the *'automatic'* and *'unconscious'* reaction. Taking a moment to compose yourself so that you can respond in an unagitated way will mean that you can keep your personal power. That's the real gold.

TAKE CHARGE

So, here's what we know. *Thoughts* and *beliefs* are forces of energy that shape or impact our lives. A thought that is directed with intention and focus repeatedly is very powerful.

Albert Einstein's definition of insanity says it perfectly: *'Insanity is doing the same thing over and over again and expecting a different result.'*

We each have an abundance of possibilities and opportunities available to us at all times. It is up to us to create the change that's needed to help us *thrive* in this life, and not merely survive.

YOUR PERSONAL RETICULAR ACTIVATING SYSTEM

One of the most powerful inbuilt tools we have for helping us as human beings is our antenna. Yes, although we're lacking the hardware – a little spike on the top of our heads, we each have an inbuilt RAS. The *'Reticular Activating System (RAS)'* functions to match and find evidence of what you are focusing on and point you in the right direction.

Have you ever noticed that when you decide to buy a new car and you have decided on a particular model, you suddenly see these types of cars everywhere on the road? All at once, seemingly out of the blue, because you've never noticed them before, now you see these cars all time! It's quite incredible. That is the RAS at work.

Considering that we have this amazing RAS that will pick up on what we're focusing on and actively help us to navigate our way to experiences and opportunities and situations that involve these intentions, I'd say that's almost reason all by itself to change some of those old limiting beliefs. Don't you?

CHAPTER 5
BREAKING DOWN FEAR

If you want something that you have never had, then you have to do something you have never done.'

BUILDING RESILIENCE AND EMBRACING YOUR FEARS

Many people avoid change and get *'stuck'* in various areas of their lives, not because they're too *lazy* to try something new, but because they're too *scared* to try something new.

However, what if I told you that fear is just an illusion? That it's all in your head.

FEAR...is False Evidence Appearing **R**eal.

Fear is not *real*. It *does not exist*.

We just *think* that fear exists.

Fear is a product of our thinking and our perception or interpretation of an outcome. Fears are just stories we tell ourselves.

The idea of fear can be innate or it can be learned.

Learned fears are fears that we take on from our parents, siblings, friends, movies or ideas we have been exposed to in the media – those strong influences from when we were growing up. Innate fears are the ones inborn in us. There's much debate around the latter, with some experts suggesting that we only have 2 legitimate innate fears: the fear of falling and fear associated with loud noises. According to this theory, all of our other fears are learned in the first several years of our life.

It's essential to realise that we can't run away from our fears forever. The more we push them away, the stronger they become and, in many cases, the more irrational they grow to be. Fears can get so out of control that they escalate into phobias, and that's when they become seriously debilitating.

Facing your fears means asking yourself what you're really afraid of.

Afterwards, ask yourself what it means.

We all mask our fears with layers of reasons and excuses that conveniently explain *why* we do what we do or *why* we are the way we are. Fears, too, can be deceiving. For example, a fear of heights is not really a fear of heights at all, but actually a fear of falling.

Take a moment and think...*what would you do if you weren't afraid?*

When you understand exactly what it is that you're afraid of and you have the courage to face it, then it no longer has any power over you. This can be wonderfully freeing.

THE 4 STEPS FOR OVERCOMING FEARS

If the primary function of our brains is to protect us, it makes sense, then, that the classic response to fear is either: *fight, freeze* or *flight*. These instant and automatic responses to fear occur in the amygdala, an almond-shaped set of neurons in the brain that are part of our limbic system which is responsible for emotions, survival instincts and memory.

Because of the brain's incredible ability to be retrained and reprogrammed successfully, it is possible to overcome fears. So, if you're ready to get started, then see if you can identify your fear on this list (it is not definitive, but it will kick-start your thinking).

Step 1: Identification

Failure	Misery	Being vulnerable
Success	Judgement (being judged)	Expressing your true feelings
Emotional pain	Not being good enough	Standing in your truth
Loneliness	Criticism	Being let down
Disappointment	Loss	Being misunderstood
Unworthiness	Intimacy	Poverty
Physical pain	Mistakes	Being reliant
Rejection	Being unloved	The unknown
Trusting others	Ridicule	Doing something different
Illness	Death	Losing your freedom

Step 2: Facing your Fear

Now it's time to ask yourself: *Why am I feeling afraid?*

- What is it that I fear?

- What problem am I facing?

- What is the real problem that I am dealing with here?

- What is the fear preventing me from doing?

- What is the fear preventing me from becoming?

- What will happen if I do nothing about it?

- What is the fear costing me emotionally, spiritually and financially?

- Why must I overcome this fear?

Step 3: Imagine life without this fear

It is important to gain clarity on what exactly it is that you would like to accomplish.

- What am I trying to accomplish?

- How will things be different once this fear is gone?

Illuminate your past and current reality. Identify your origin of fear, past experience and fear triggers.

- How did this fear originate?

- When did this fear begin?

- How long has this fear persisted?

- Have I experienced this fear before?

- How did I overcome the fear?

- How did I fail to overcome the fear?

- When do I feel this fear? Under what circumstances?

- What specifically triggers this fear in me?

- What aspects of this fear do I control?

- What aspects don't I control?

- Are these real or simply imagined?

- How could I potentially gain control over these aspects?

- What are the biggest obstacles standing in my way?

- How will I overcome these obstacles?

- What resources do I have that could be of value here?

- How could I use them to assist me?

Step 4: Eliminate the fear

Ask yourself:

- Does this fear make any sense?

- How is this fear absolutely crazy and absurd?

- As a matter of fact, what is funny about this fear that I hadn't realised before?

- How would I approach this fear from the perspective of an artist? Celebrity? Politician? Entrepreneur? Scientist?

- What's the first step I would take to overcome this fear?

- What's the next step I would take?

When you thoroughly understand what fears exist within you and why, then ask yourself:

- What are the consequences of keeping this fear?

- What will happen if I do nothing about this fear?

- What is this fear really costing me?

Take time over this and really engage because the more strongly you can connect with your imagination and the feeling of liberation that will result when you change this fear, the easier it will be to make the transition.

VISUALISE AND MATERIALISE

Because our mind cannot tell the difference; the clearer your vision and the stronger your emotional connection is to this picture in your head, the higher the likelihood of success.

> *"Courage is resistance to fear, mastery of fear, not absence of fear."*–
> **Mark Twain**

You might strike obstacles, so deal with them as you move through the process. Remember that you have everything within you to make significant and permanent change, it just takes 21 days.

Journaling helps too. Think about the reasons you purchased this book and what you learned about yourself so far.

DREAM BIG; DON'T LET FEAR GET IN THE WAY

What do you think is the number one obstacle that stands in the way of most people and their dreams? Because we've been talking so much about fear, you probably think it is fear. Or, perhaps doubt, lack of confidence, lack of inspiration, no motivation, no money or lack of opportunity.

Actually, it is none of the above.

The real reason is that we get side-tracked.

A lot of us lose sight of our dreams this way. Yes, life is busy with conflicting priorities, other responsibilities and circumstances, all competing for our attention; diverting our energy, minute-by-minute, day-by-day. Nevertheless, we should never let our goals escape our grasp.

Here's the thing: once you take the first step, you're already halfway there. The beginning is the biggest hurdle you will ever be faced with. Once you've taken the plunge and put faith in yourself, the opportunities will present themselves.

Piece by piece after you've demonstrated your own commitment to the idea or process that you want to pursue, you can begin to create a new life, make new decisions and carve out a new destiny.

That's not to say that during this journey there won't be emotional challenges, impediments, snags, stumbling blocks and setbacks, all of which can create confusion. However, they are only put in your path to test your will and to strengthen your resolve. Alongside these difficult times, there will also be exciting opportunities, wonderful changes, good fortune, hope and freedom.

If you are clear about what you want, then circumstances and situations that align with this goal will present themselves. Remember your RAS? It needs to be supported by your own undertaking – your own hard work and diligence.

While you might have doubts and fears in the beginning, it's important to keep perspective. If you let them *persist*, then they will cloud your vision and warp the signals that you're projecting to yourself and others about your successful new life, which is built on faith in yourself connected with *passion* and *purpose*. If you remain focused on the fear, then the distractions will return, keeping you bogged down on a path that doesn't make your heart sing or fulfil your soul.

GOOD THINGS CAN BE BAD THINGS

Another aspect that gets in the way of our dreams is not the *'bad things'* we are faced with, but the *'good things'* that keeps us in our comfort zone and doesn't require us to change or challenge the status quo.

Kahlil Gibran, the author of *'The Prophet'*, explains that we all come into this world with our purpose in our heart. All we need to do is connect with it, focus upon it and allow ourselves to be driven by it. That is how we will find success.

Nonetheless, living life with this kind of single-minded motivation is not easy.

Fear and doubt are ever present around us. If we let them, they can create clutter and heaviness in the heart. To overcome fear and doubt, you have to transform them into courage and action.

Action breeds confidence and conquers fear!

Conquering fear is possible because fear is only a figment of our imaginations.

Like all things that we imagine, we can change it according to our heart's desire. In our mind's eye, we can see things differently and experience things differently.

If you have a dream to chase, then write it down. Memorise it. *See* those words in your head when you're focusing on it.

> *"The only thing that stands between you and your dream is the will to try and to believe that it is actually possible."* – **Joel Brown**

BEWARE OF WHAT YOU TELL YOURSELF

Language shapes the way we think. From early childhood, we learn to frame our experiences with words, an essential aspect for communicating with each other. We learn by mimicking the world around us – labelling objects, feelings and experiences so that we can express what we are thinking. At an early age, we don't really give much consideration to the words themselves.

However, words are very powerful. And so is the tone they are spoken in. Words are a clue as to what is going on in your unconscious mind and your beliefs. This is why it is of great importance to speak impeccably so to be conscious of your words to create the change you want to be.

- *What's your story?*
- *What are you telling yourself?*
- *How are you feeding your fear?*

It's critical to realise that our unconscious mind believes whatever we are told – we are selfish, or naughty, or lazy, or beautiful, or clever, or kind.

Words can be emotional triggers from our past experiences too. For instance, for someone who has a memory bank full of idyllic childhood moments spent at the beach, the association with the word *beach* will be much more positive than it is likely to be for someone who got badly stung by a jellyfish, lost in crowd or pulled under by a big wave at the beach.

Words also carry energy. Even though the spoken word is gone in a moment, the energy of words can linger indefinitely.

Words can be enlightening. They can make us feel sad, they can make us feel happy and they can make us feel empowered. Words can inspire or deflate.

Most of the time, we're pretty careful about the words we choose to say to other people. After all, we want people to like us, so we are usually polite and considerate.

Sadly, we do not tend to extend this courtesy to ourselves. Instead, our self-talk is usually along the lines of:

- I can't
- I should
- I could
- I will try
- I must
- I might
- I ought to
- I have to
- I am supposed to

What kind of energy do these words carry? Just by reading the list you can tell that they are not motivating, inspiring or persuasive. There is no commitment; the words carry the energy that you are moving away from the very thing you aspire to be, have or do.

By making a conscious effort to swap these words around to:

- I can
- I will
- I want
- I choose
- I select
- I decide
- I am able

You can begin to create the shift required to change those unhelpful, old, unconscious thought patterns and help you get to where you want to be.

It's a subtle, but a significant shift, and it will provide noticeable benefits to the way you feel about yourself and the life you are living.

I have to or *I really must* imply pressure and obligation. On the other hand, by saying *I can* or *I will* suggest that there are opportunities, choices and options.

Like all of the changes we've discussed in this book, consciously choosing your words will take time and practice. But understanding how much power words can wield is a good start. Changing your words will change your outcomes.

"Words can inspire and words can destroy. Choose yours well." – **Robin Sharma**

CHAPTER 6
CREATING THE RIGHT MINDSET FOR CHANGE

'Let go of the familiar, do something different every day. To create something new, you have to forget your old self.'

THE 3 LAYERS OF THE BRAIN

It's time for a brief lesson in biology.

Did you know that we have 3 brains? Yes – 3 brains!

Neuroscientist Paul McLean coined the term **Triune Brain** to describe them.

The Lizard Brain

The first layer of your brain is the *lizard brain* or reptilian brain; this is where the unconscious mind resides. It developed earliest in our evolution and it manages:

- Repetitive tasks
- Motor skills
- Action selection
- Physical survival and safety
- Immediate fear response

This part of the brain controls the heart and the breath. It is compulsive, and it is always active, even during sleep.

The *lizard* part of the brain is the part that responds to *pain* and *pleasure*. It makes this distinction very simple: *pain* is to be avoided (identify undesirable behaviour) and *pleasure* is to be pursued (identify desired behaviour).

It is essential to understand this when you want to change bad habits and old patterns or behaviours, because this is the part of the brain that responds when you begin to work on creating new habits over 21 days.

Furthermore, because the *lizard* part of your brain includes your unconscious mind (which is like a 5–7-year-old child and is sometimes referred to as the *inner child*), it responds to the simple language of pictures and symbols rather than complex words and phrases. This is why it is attracted to vision boards, and it is also why vision boards work really well when you are creating your goals.

The Monkey Brain

The second layer is called the *monkey brain* or the limbic part of your brain. There's quite a lot that goes on in this area of the brain. Emotion is generated here and this section of the brain also manages:

- Instinct
- Freeze, fight or flight response
- Long-term memory

The *monkey* part of our brain governs relationships, attachment and the nervous response that triggers our emotions. This second layer also responds to reward. It seeks *approval* and *punishment*. It avoids judgement. Desired outcomes are rewarded and celebrated, and undesired outcomes are punished and disciplined. This part of the brain is where we process *cause* and *effect*.

Processing *cause* and *effect* is critical in our interactions with others. A lot of people spend their whole lives blaming others. You've probably met people like this – victims of life, circumstance and relationships. *Why-always-me* types. It would seem they are just never able to take responsibility for themselves and stop repeating old mistakes.

Understanding *cause* and *effect* is critical to owning up to your actions and being able to see very clearly that we are not only responsible for things that happen to us, but we actually have a very large degree of control over what happens too.

Random acts do occur, but basically, right now, this is your life to lead as you please.

We are *at cause* for every reaction we get from other people, so if you don't like the response or reaction that you receive, it's the perfect moment to ask yourself, *What did I do to cause that?*

For every action, there is a reaction. At a basic scientific level this is, quite simply, energy exchange.

<u>Cause</u> is the <u>reason</u> why something happens, and <u>effect</u> is the <u>result</u>.

For example:

- Caroline missed her train (effect) because she slept in (cause).
- Sam didn't read the Ikea instructions correctly (cause) so the table was lop-sided (effect).
- Tom received a speeding fine (effect) because he was driving 80 km in a 60 km zone (cause).

We process this in the monkey part of the brain. Once we fully comprehend it, we can take complete ownership of our own actions, and subsequent reactions. We can also begin to appreciate the energetic flow of *cause* and *effect* working within our lives.

The *monkey* part of our brain is also where repressed memories and unresolved negative emotions reside. If you do not take the time to acknowledge and change these, you will continue to run these old programs or limiting beliefs. The monkey brain will continue to find evidence to support whatever it is you want to focus on, whether it is something wanted or unwanted. As a result, the frustrations in your life will continue to repeat; a bit like the Bill Murray movie, *Groundhog Day*.

The Human Brain

The third and final layer of our brain is the pre-frontal cortex or neo-cortex, which McLean refers to as the *human brain*. This is the conscious mind that houses:

- Will power
- Analyses
- Thinking
- Observations
- Problem-solving

- Planning
- Reasoning

The *human brain* processes all the data that comes through our 5 senses; this is where conscious thought and Meta cognition takes place.

The *human brain* responds to self-improvement, self-direction and transcendent purpose. This part of the brain thrives on going beyond the limits – surpassing or exceeding ordinary experiences. Now, that's an exciting place to be!

However, when we are *stressed*, the *monkey brain* becomes overactive – it won't allow us to plan, reason or solve our problems because it will hijack our pre-frontal cortex.

This is another reason why it is so important to take time each day to connect the head and the heart – through silence, meditation, sport or whatever enables us to *let go of the daily strains* to ensure healthy brain function.

INTELLECT AND MOTIVATION

To be able to break old habits, and in doing so, create long-lasting change, we must understand how all 3 brains work and relate with each other.

Let's have a look how this may work using intellect and motivation.

First, identify the behaviour that you wish to change and link it to significant *pain*. Remember, your *lizard brain* will avoid pain and try to run away from it, so the stronger the connection to *pain*, the better the outcome.

Next, identify your *desired* behaviour and link massive *pleasure* to it. Your *lizard brain* will pursue pleasure and, if you bring in an emotional connection, you will allow the *lizard* and *monkey brain* to work together by *increasing* and *intensifying* that feeling.

Now, let's put it into context.

We will begin by adding *significant pain*.

Let's say one of my behaviours that I would like to change is that I always say 'YES' to everything and everyone – to the point where it's detrimental to me, my business and my success. To add enough significant pain, I would be saying to myself that, if I continue to act out this behaviour, I will no longer be in business. How would that make me feel? I would intensify these feelings with the loss of my work that I love so very much and the loss of my customers etc. I am guessing you know what I mean if you can resonate with something that is of a great loss.

The next step is to add a desired behaviour and link *massive pleasure*.

For example, my desired behaviour would be the practice of saying 'NO'. Doing so would allow me more time to focus and spend time on my customers and business to see them grow and bloom into something wonderful. To intensify this with emotion, I would feel elevated and evoke immense satisfaction on completing my entire tasks and be of service.

Now you can make the change by working out a process for moving forward. As you do, make sure you reward each step of the way. Share your progress with your friends and family; let them know you are doing well. Your *monkey brain* loves reward.

By making it public, by sharing it with your friends and family, it creates more accountability, which in turn creates better results.

While you're going through this process, it is possible that you will encounter resistance or triggers that might take you backwards. Some people might say, "*three steps forward, one step back*"...others call this the "*Cha Cha*". It's all a process – you cannot rush it and you cannot predict it, but it is important that you stay positive and surround yourself with supportive people and energy.

Keep it up for 21 days, so that your new change becomes an ingrained habit.

MINDFULNESS

To be mindful is to bring your full attention to the present moment. It is about paying attention in a particular way – fully experiencing the moment – without judgement or expectation. Mindfulness is about being conscious, bringing complete awareness to your *here right now* experience, with openness and receptiveness.

The benefits of mindfulness are many. First and foremost, it helps you to improve your focus and concentration. This is crucial when you want to manifest abundance or changes in your life, relationships or career.

Mindfulness also assists in *reflection* and *self-awareness*. By doing so, it helps you facilitate better relationships. By practicing mindfulness on a daily basis – for as little as 10 minutes a day until you have the ability to do it longer – you will experience less stress, your emotions will become less volatile and you will find an ability to calmly and sensibly solve the problems in your life more easily and without distraction.

Additionally, mindfulness will help you to turn your attention on those unwanted beliefs or self-sabotaging patterns that you unconsciously run over and over again. It will aid you in identifying them so that you can change them.

You can achieve mindfulness in a few easy steps:

1) Stop and just be – pause.

2) Pay attention.

- What do you hear?
- How do you feel?
- What's happening in your environment?

3) Observe without judgment.

- What are the common patterns that you recognise?

4) Question – Ask yourself:

- Why do you do this?
- Does a response pop into your head?

5) Associate – Join the dots to find out where this behaviour comes from (most of the times they are old beliefs that no longer serve you):

- Self-worth
- Self-drive
- Self-esteem
- Self-acceptance
- Self-denial
- Self-respect
- Self-confidence
- Self-belief
- Self-doubt
- Or Self-love

6) Journal – record and write all of your experiences during the process. Sometimes writing things down will give you another perspective on reality.

Then, when you're ready to create change, here are 5 things you can do to make it happen!

Disassociate. Close your eyes and imagine that you're a superhero removing your armour. This visual will help you to disconnect and separate yourself from the behaviour.

Reframe. Change the content or the context (as discussed in Chapter 1). Think of new ways you could behave or new beliefs you could replace the old ones with.

Take 10 Breaths. Once you have the reframed image in your mind and you can see it as clearly as possible, close your eyes. Concentrate on feeling the emotions associated with the new change – excitement, joy, happiness, peace, whatever it may be. Add sound too – laughter, tone of voice. Capture and crystallise the new content with all of these effects, making it as real as possible so that you begin to physically experience it, rather than just see it in your imagination.

Mantras and autosuggestions can help to set the right intentions or *headspace* for the day ahead. You might say something like: *'I am strong and safe'* or *'I have the power to transform my life'* or *'I am at peace with change'*. Make it personal. Give it meaning – perhaps add a colour or an image or see the words in your head when you think of them. Keep it simple so that you can conjure it up quickly and comfortably. When the negative thought pops into your head or the anxious feelings creep into your belly; use the mantra until you feel calm and back on track. Use it as often as you can or when you need to.

Meditation. Get comfortable, either seated or lying down. Create a space that you love and feel peaceful in. You might choose music. You might choose darkness or candlelight, or sunshine under a big tree in a garden. It's entirely up to you. The point of meditation is to *'clear the mind'*. However, because actually cultivating the ability to think of nothing is very difficult to achieve and takes many hours of practice, people feel like they don't get the benefits of meditation and therefore, they do not do it.

Benefits of meditation

'Calming' or *'quieting the mind'* is a lot easier to achieve and is just as beneficial. Anything that slows us down, and which helps to unclutter our minds, is a counteraction to the busy lives we lead. It's good for our emotional, physical and spiritual health. CDs, phone apps, YouTube videos are all useful – whatever helps you to achieve a relaxed state where you can let your thoughts just *'be'* without getting tangled up is a very good thing!

It is more beneficial to do 10 minutes of meditation daily than it is to do a one-hour session per week. Meditation helps us to live consciously and purposefully and with personal integrity. It is the greatest tool we have at our disposal for connecting the head and the heart and the soul, so it's a great skill to learn.

The benefits of meditation are numerous. Meditation:

- Releases fear
- Release stress and tension
- Reduces anxiety
- Relaxes the nervous system
- Relieves muscle tension
- Relieves insomnia
- Increase concentration and the ability to focus
- Increase energy and motivation
- Improve memory
- Reduces depression
- Lowers blood pressure
- Normalises blood pressure
- Reduces cholesterol levels that decrease the risk of cardiovascular disease
- Slows down your cardiovascular system
- Restores balanced function to the digestive system, aiding absorption of nutrients
- Diminishes intensity of headaches or migraines
- And it frees your mind from self-doubt and internal chatter

Try this:

Visualise a white light coming into the crown of your head. Imagine it filling up all of the space in your head and moving through your body, down your neck, your torso, arms, fingers, belly, back, thighs, calves, feet, toes. Imagine this light filling you up slowly, so that you have time to concentrate on each area of your body. If your concentration breaks, gently bring it back to where you were. If you feel pain or any kind of sensation, focus on this area, imagine the white light radiating around this spot. Acknowledge whatever feelings, emotions, sensations come up.

It might help to keep a journal handy so that when you've finished your meditation, you can note these down to consider later.

Meditation practiced daily can generate:

- Optimism
- Self-esteem
- Confidence
- Motivation
- Self-acceptance
- Self-responsibility
- Self-assertiveness

BRAIN WAVES

Brain waves are the way that neurons in our brains communicate. Like radio waves, they have different frequencies, depending on what we're doing and what we're feeling. When the slower brainwaves are dominant, we can feel tired, slow and sluggish. When we feel alert, higher frequencies are dominant.

Gamma. These are the fastest of all brainwaves and are associated with peak performance or that amazing *'in-the-zone'* feeling that you can do anything. Neuroscientists tell us, we can achieve such state by focusing on love and compassion, or the things we absolutely love to do.

Beta. When we are wide-awake – and in a normal, alert state – this frequency is active. Being in this state for too long can lead to anxiety, stress, panic and even disease, so it's important to actively find the space to relax from time to time, so your Alpha brainwaves can take over from Beta.

Alpha. These brainwaves are active when we are calm and relaxed. This is one of the best vibrations to be in. It increases serotonin levels (which is the chemical in the brain responsible for happiness). What's more, this frequency helps you to sleep better and can relieve anxiety and depression. Even more so, it can boost your creative visualisation.

Theta. Brainwaves produce a deep state of relaxation and meditation. In this state, we have enhanced creativity and problem-solving skills and can access the unconscious mind. Most individuals access this brainwave through hypnosis or when we are in the dream state that is REM sleep.

Delta. Dreamless sleep and deep trance. In this state you have no body awareness and access to the collective unconscious mind. You are naturally in this frequency when you are in a deep sleep – your body restores and human growth hormones are released. This is why it is so important to get a good night's rest.

HAVING THE RIGHT MINDSET

To achieve, you must first believe. But if you don't believe, then how can you shift your thinking?

Well, you have to **Pretend** and **Practice**, until you **Perfect** it. These are the 3 Ps you need to create change. Remember, you have the ability and all of the resources you need to achieve *anything* you want to; you just have to open your mind a little, imagine and visualise.

Let's say, for argument's sake, that your goal is to have more *self-worth*.

The first step is: Pretend.

Imagine having it right now. What would it feel like if you had *self-worth*? Close your eyes and visualise it – captivating, confidence, charisma? Find the words to describe what it means to you, then give them a meaning and feeling and write it down.

Next, while still visualising that you have *self-worth*:

- What does it look like for you?
- What is around you?
- What can you hear?
- What do you see?
- How do you feel?
- How are others reacting to you?
- How does your voice sound?

Be as descriptive as you can – you're painting a picture in your mind. Now, give your picture a word or a sentence.

Finally, consider your beliefs. What are your beliefs around your goal? Do you believe that you can achieve *self-worth*? Of course, you can!

Uh oh...negative response? Don't worry, that just means you're going to have to work harder to get rid of that first. Go over the first 2 steps until you're confident you can move on.

Now you have a list of words or sentences that you can use to create a statement or affirmation.

For instance, let's pretend that you came up with the following:

- I feel joy and excitement.
- I hear laughter.
- I see my loved ones smiling as I accept and value all that is around me.
- Opportunities and love are more common now than ever before in history, and I believe that it is possible that with my talent, I can create the life and abundance that I have always dreamt about.

Moving on, using these words and sentences, your statement/affirmation might look something like this:

> '*I am happy; I am worthy and deserve all that life has to offer me. I am strong and I am perfect just the way that I am. I love myself for*

who I am. I am good enough! I feel such joy and excitement with what I will create.'

The next P stands for *Practice*.

Now that you have your statement, practice, practice, practice. As often as possible, day and night, on the bus, waiting for the traffic lights, in the shower, while you're jogging. Make it your yoga mantra. Say it over and over and over again. Make sure that you really connect with the feeling of having it *now*. It is your current experience; not something to wait for, not something that has been. It is now.

With lots of effective practice, you will get to the final P – *Perfection*! This is where you have achieved your goal and you can congratulate yourself.

You're amazing.

> *"Faith is to believe what you do not see; the reward of this faith is to see what you believe."* – **Saint Augustine**

CHAPTER 7
Unleash Your Inner Courage

'Every day is a second chance. Take a chance in the unknown.'

STANDING IN YOUR TRUTH

To stand in your truth is to stand in your true power and accept everything that you are, as well as everything you are not.

It means embracing your essence, taking off your mask and not caring about what other people think.

It is about forging an authentic connection with yourself and truly understanding yourself.

When you stand in your own truth, you not only discover your incredible potential, but you also find total freedom.

- Are you a people pleaser?
- Are you a 'yes' person?
- Are you afraid to say 'no'?
- Do you avoid having courageous conversations?

If you answered yes to any of the above questions, then you're probably wondering how you might break these old patterns and create the necessary change for you to be completely comfortable in your own skin. More than that, you would like to continue day by day to be the best version of yourself that you can possibly be.

Quite simply, the most important person in your universe is you. Frankly, it *is* all about you. If you are not happy or content, it will have a knock-on effect with your partner, children, loved ones, work, and business, more importantly, it will have a huge impact on *your* life.

One of the greatest lessons we can learn is to treat ourselves with the respect that we show others. Perhaps then, the second greatest lesson that we can learn is that unless we put ourselves first, and meet our own needs and desires, then we cannot possibly be of service to others.

This may sound *'selfish'* but it's not. It's being self-full.

We've all experienced countless moments when we have said *'yes'* when we really meant *'no'*. What's more, most times the *'yes'* we say to others comes at the cost of saying *'no'* to ourselves. More often than not, this old pattern has a lot to do with how we feel about ourselves – our self-worth and our need to be liked or approved of, or not judged by other people.

Just imagine: if you had a special superpower where you could say all of the things you wanted to without being afraid.

Well, you do have that superpower. It is called *'courage'*, and for it to work effectively, you must also use it with *'compassion'*.

You need the courage to stand in your own truth. To understand what you need and not be afraid to say it. You need compassion to send this message to other people when they are asking for things of you that you cannot possibly deliver.

Most of us get caught up in being reactionary, especially if we are feeling defensive, angry, uncertain or anything else. Standing in your truth and speaking from the heart requires you to be responsive, not reactionary. There's a big difference.

Pause, take a breath, summon compassion, love and kindness, and your words will reflect this energy and intention.

Therefore, while you're reading this and still shaking in your shoes at the idea of telling your boss you can't possibly take on another project with your current workload, you must also be a little curious. You should wonder what would happen if you actually had this conversation and said what you wanted to say, in good faith, trusting that your boss would understand that you're speaking from the heart.

Let me tell you a secret: the outcome will be perfect.

Most people consider it honourable when you speak your mind, especially if you do it kindly. If your boss doesn't think this, then perhaps this is a **really big flashing neon sign** to suggest that you might take a look at whether your job is the right one for you.

Either way, trust that the outcome puts you exactly where you are meant to be at this point in time. Hug yourself and be proud of yourself. Whether or not this really matters to you, know that for someone, somewhere in your sphere, you are a role model and you just showed them how to take one of the most important steps on the path to self-respect.

Stand up for what you believe in, even if it means standing alone.

We will never get what we ask for with thoughts and feelings alone. Yes, we can say mantras to change our mindset. Yes, we can visualise and hone our RAS (Reticular Activating System). These are important, but it is *action* that really creates momentum.

Once you are courageous enough to stand in your truth at a time when it counts, you take action. With the support of all you visualise and mantra-cise, these actions will kick-start your brand new life.

You will find the kind of serenity that comes from knowing that you are being your *authentic self*. You are now *'walking your talk'*.

When you *stand in your truth*, you treat yourself with the same consideration that you would give someone else. You treat yourself with respect. You honour yourself for the way in which you are moving forward. You become your best friend and supporter. You focus on your positive attributes and build on them.

You are far too smart to be the only thing standing in your way. –
Jennifer J. Freeman

COURAGEOUS CONVERSATIONS

We often wonder *why* our conversations fail whether they are difficult, courageous or growth conversations.

When communicating this aspect, the reality of it all is that we are not prepared and we have not planned for these conversations. The list below shows some of the reasons *why* our conversations may be challenging.

The key here is this: the drivers of these conversations come in from different directions. For example, a *difficult* conversation, the driver of the conversation comes from an external event, situation or circumstance. Whereas the driver for a *courageous* conversation, the feeling and driving force comes from within, it's an internal drive. A growth conversation can be external as feedback to light up your blind spot or internal where you know you need to expand on your self-awareness to work more with your strengths. Or focus on your goals to get to your desired aspiration. Mind you, there is grey in some of these drivers; let's say I was to pull you up on your behaviour, this may be initially a difficult conversation for me and a growth conversation for you.

Difficult	**Courageous**	**Growth**
✓ Uncomfortable	✓ I Love you	✓ Encouraging
✓ Topic specific	✓ Accountability	✓ Blind spots
✓ Honesty	✓ Self-evaluation	✓ Strengths
✓ The other person	✓ Opportunities	✓ Asking questions
✓ Fear of reaction	✓ Telling the truth	✓ Clarity
✓ Managing Performance	✓ Uncomfortable	✓ Goals
✓ Empathy	✓ Managing up	✓ Emotional
✓ Confidence	✓ Trust	✓ Pro-active
✓ Agreement	✓ Standing in your truth	✓ Plan
✓ Conflict	✓ Asking for help	✓ Risk
✓ Position	✓ Vulnerability	✓ Change
✓ External behaviour	✓ Exposing one's thoughts	✓ Discovery
		✓ Engagement

So...how do we prepare for our courageous conversation?

First, you have to prepare and really think hard about *what the purpose or outcome of this conversation is.*

It has to be one simple sentence.

For example, the outcome of my courageous conversation is that I have more time for me and that I feel there is balance in my relationship.

Write a list down of some of the key points you would like to bring up in your courageous conversation.

For instance, my list may look like this:

- Cleaning
- Cooking
- Washing
- Grocery shopping
- Time

To highlight the concept, here is a detailed example: my relationship in my eyes may not be a level playing field, or it may not be balanced. This is hypothetical, of course, but let's say that I am always doing all the cleaning, cooking, washing and grocery shopping. This would mean that I never have time for myself, while my partner is out every night gallivanting, taking no responsibilities around house chores.

I would then turn those points into questions. Why, you may ask? Well, if you are just sitting there across from your partner pointing out all these topics you want to cover, what do you think will be the outcome of your courageous conversation?

Absolute disaster! Yes...nobody likes to be dictated to, nor does anyone like to have what they are not doing right to be pointed out to them especially when they are well aware of what they are not doing!

Imagine though, if your partner was to come up with all the insights and solutions him or herself. What do you think the outcome of your courageous conversation is going to be like then?

Correct! One of great success, result and resolution. So, how does it go?

Turning your points into questions – *Why? What* and *How?*

- Cleaning –

  o Why is cleaning important to you?
  o What is cleaning to you?
  o How do you clean?

- Cooking –

  o Why is cooking important?
  o What is cooking to you?
  o How do you cook?

- Washing –

  o Why is washing important?
  o What is washing to you?
  o How do you do the washing?

- Grocery shopping –

  o Why are groceries important?
  o What are groceries to you?
  o How do you get groceries?

- Time –

  o Why is spending time for you important?
  o What is spending time for you mean to you?
  o How do you spend time for you?

The power of getting to the *why* is all unconscious – it is *why* we do or do not do the things that are expected of us. It gives us insight into what the other person's drivers are and a deeper understanding without pointing the finger at anyone.

When communicating, be conscious to use positive words. Furthermore, when you plan your courageous conversation, I would highly recommend to typing it up and turning those negative words into positive words for an amicable outcome.

THE SECRET TO SAYING *NO*

If you've ever spent any time with a toddler, you'll notice that they say 'No' a lot. In developmental terms, this is a big milestone and it happens around the age of 2–3 years. A recent study actually found that toddlers argue with their parents as much as 20–25 times per hour! The important fact here is that toddlers are not doing this to be difficult and defy parental authority. For them, it's more about exerting a sense of self and a sense of control in their little worlds where everything is new and can be bit overwhelming.

Adults can learn a thing or 2 from this. Relocating this sense of self is a good start.

Saying 'no' is hard. You don't want to be seen as rude, or difficult or unhelpful. So, don't give people reason to think that at all. Smile, and politely say one of these alternatives:

- Can I get back to you?
- Can I think about it?
- Unfortunately, it's not a good time right now.
- Maybe another time.
- Sounds great, but I have other commitments.
- Could you please give me more information before I decide?
- Thank you, but no thank you.
- I'd love to, but I can't.
- Thank you for thinking of me, but I can't.
- Another time might be better.
- I'm not sure if I am the best person for it.
- I'm trying to cut back on commitments.

- I won't be able to dedicate the extra time needed for this project.

SETTING PERSONAL BOUNDARIES

From an early age, we are taught to identify and create reasonable, safe and permissible ways for others to behave around us. It's really important to set personal boundaries with others.

Why?

Because some people are time wasters and some people are energy drainers. Some people zap our sense of *'self'*, and that doesn't leave us feeling great.

The critical part to remember here is that people only treat you one way, the way you allow them to. Setting personal boundaries helps us to understand that no one can make us feel anything unless we allow them to. Furthermore, it gives us essential guidelines as to what we will accept and what we will not tolerate.

Here's an exercise that will help you to understand your boundaries.

Complete these sentences to create physical (how we act), emotional (how we feel) and mental (how we think) boundaries.

For example:

I am a very private person.

I am not very open about my feelings.

I want freedom.

I do not want people taking over.

I will speak my mind.

I will not allow someone to take advantage of me.

You try it now and see what insights you get from this exercise.

I AM

_____

I AM NOT

_____

I WANT

_____

I DO NOT WANT

_____

I WILL

_____

I WILL NOT

_____

> *"Boundaries are a part of self-care. They are healthy, normal and necessary."* – **Doreen Virtue**

YOUR CIRCLE OF POWER

There are times in life when we all need a boost; a bit more power.

I'm going to tell you a way that you can create some, just at the times when you need it the most. The circle of power will help you to manifest more:

- Self-worth

- Self-trust
- Self-esteem
- Self-love
- Self-care
- Self-confidence
- Self-fullness
- Self-awareness

So, instead of feeling:

- Fear
- Nervous
- Unconfident
- Unworthy

You will be instantly able to feel:

- Powerful
- Confident
- Fearless
- Motivated

The most wonderful part about the circle of power is that you take it with you wherever you go and you bring it out when you need it most.

Your circle of power is your magical circle. With the right intention, imagination, belief, visualisation and the *right energy* – these each combine to create a powerful circle. The more you use your circle, the more powerful it becomes. The more attention, energy and focus that go into your circle, the more you will create into your reality. Focused attention results in attracting exactly what you want.

This is how you can design your own circle:

1. Decide what your circle's special power will be. For example, let's use self-worth.

2. Imagine a circle of power in front of you. It's about 2 feet or 60 cm in diameter.
3. Remember a time when you felt totally worthy. It doesn't matter the circumstance or how long ago the memory; just really bring it to life. Connect with it and escalate the feeling as strongly as you can.
4. Stack it on. Think of other times when you felt really worthy, and place them in the circle too. The more experiences you can stack, the stronger your circle will be.
5. Admire your stack of experiences. See them, hear them, and feel them. Magnify them and increase the intensity and then step into your circle of power and soak up the energy.
6. Add colour if you want to, or a soundtrack, a song that makes you feel everything you want to in the circle.
7. Step into your circle of power, when you are at your peak, intensify them even more. Feel the powerful emotion surrounding you and flowing through your body.
8. Now anchor this feeling with a word or phrase – *'"I am worthy and so much more'* – and anchor that emotion on your physiology, like your earlobe as an example.
9. Stay in your circle of power as long as you need to. Keep building on your emotions until you are feeling euphoric and with an abundance of self-worth.
10. Before the intensity fades, step out of your circle of power. You can repeat this exercise as often as you feel the need, the circle becomes more powerful.

Keep it in mind to use at times when you feel nervous or stressed, such as a:

- Meeting
- Interview
- Courageous conversation
- Telephone call
- First day at work or school

Just visualise it in front of you and step into your circle of power, firing all your anchors. Have fun with it! Remember, what you visualise will materialise.

LIFE IS ABOUT BALANCE AND HARMONY

The existence of balance is everywhere. There is no up without a down, a good without a bad, and a success without a failure and so on. It's a world of duality and dichotomy.

Everything has a duality. We have female and male in us, we have positive and negative in us. Opposites are identical in nature, just like the Ying and Yang.

The concept is easy to understand, but how do we master the art of balance?

It takes single-minded focus on you and what you can control.

Forget what you cannot control, that is a waste of your time and energy.

Detach yourself from an outcome or expectation. Let the situation unfold and surprise you!

If you don't like surprises, then at least understand that *'what will be, will be'*. All you can do is get on with what you're doing, and trust the process.

> **The Universal Laws:**
>
> **Law of Vibration and Attraction.** You, my friend, are a magnet. Everything you are thinking or feeling is being transmitted to the world around you. Because everything else has energy and is affected by your energy, what you send out, you will receive back. According to the law of vibration and attraction, what you focus on is what you will receive.

Law of Perpetual Transmutation of Energy. This is all about change. Change is constant. Nothing in the world is permanent. Change is inevitable. We all have the power to experience change and effect change.

Law of Action. Nothing happens without energy and movement. If you want to work towards reaching a goal, if you want to change your life, the most important step is the first one.

Law of Correspondence. Your outer world is a reflection of your inner world. Basically, this means that you are the creator of your reality. Perception is projection. Believe it, achieve it, live it.

Law of Cause and Effect. With every action = Cause, there is a reaction = Effect. What you sow is what you reap. It is far more empowering to be 'at cause' rather than constantly making excuses because you're living on the 'effect' side of this equation. To be at cause is to be responsible and accountable for all your actions! This law teaches us that nothing happens by chance; we create it no matter what the circumstances.

Law of Relativity. Nothing is good or bad until we relate it to something or compare it to something or someone else. Life exists by comparison, whether it's good/bad, hot/cold, poor/rich or big/small. When we look at life and believe that 'it is, what it is' instead of comparing or relating it to something else, life is simple. And really, there's no need to complicate it. Remember, everything has the meaning we give it. So, when there are obstacles in our path, we can either accept them for what they are or look at them in a different light. Everything is an opportunity for growth and we have the power to change our ways of interpretation.

Law of Polarity. Everything has an opposite. Just like the Yin and Yang symbol, positive can't exist without you experiencing the negative, happiness can't exist without you experiencing sadness and success can't exist without you experiencing failure. This law teaches us that everything has an opposite – the key to becoming a master is to have a perfect balance between the polarities.

Law of Rhythm. Think of the tides of the ocean, the sunrise, the sunset, and the seasons. Everything has a rhythm to it that creates harmony. Learning to understand our own rhythm – when we need to dance, and run, and when we need to eat, rest and meditate – helps us to be productive and to find peace and calm in our lives. In times of adversity, we should see the lesson and remember that *'this too, shall pass.'*

CHAPTER 8
UNIVERSAL LAWS OF HARMONY

'Once you make a decision, the whole universe collaborates to make it happen.'

WHAT ARE YOUR GUIDING PRINCIPLES?

Principles are described as rules or laws that are universal in nature. They are our foundation blocks. They're our rules, our moral compass. Principles drive our predictions and our actions, and they give us boundaries to operate within when we interrelate with each other.

Values are a set of beliefs about right or wrong, good or bad and appropriate or inappropriate. Values serve as a guiding force in life and provide a sense of direction.

Why understanding principles and values is critical

When it comes to *happiness*, understanding your principles is fundamental. Your values determine what you do with your time and how you evaluate and validate the time you have spent on these activities. Principles are motivators and give us a purpose for getting up in the morning. They also tend to be the measures we use to determine whether or not our lives are turning out the way we want them to be.

Your values influence your:

- Behaviours
- Attitudes
- Choices
- Goals
- Emotions
- Motivations
- Judgments
- Habits
- Lifestyle
- Social experience

When the things we do and the way we behave match our values, life is usually good, right? We are satisfied and content. But when these don't align with our values, that's when things feel...wrong. This can be a real source of unhappiness.

Principles exist, whether we want to recognise them or not. Life is much easier when we acknowledge them, value them and make decisions that honour them.

When we know a little about another person's values, we can work out what's important to them. We can understand what motivates them and we are better able to connect in a more meaningful and authentic way because we have a greater insight into this person and their actions.

Often, our values are our filter when it comes to the way we view the world around us. For example, if your top priority is family, then family is what you will consider highly with regard to any actions or decisions you need to make. If your priority is health, then it will be a primary driver. Different circumstances call for different drivers. For example, in business – making money might score highly on the list for some people, and for others it might be *'creating a balanced lifestyle'*. In complex situations, sometimes priorities can conflict. This is when we really need to take time to connect with ourselves to figure out what is going to be the most important.

Values and principles can also change over time, depending on circumstances and events in your life. A serious illness, having children or the loss of a family member can all affect the values that we place priority upon.

Let's explore some examples.

Relationships

If you value intimacy and companionship, and your partner values solitude and doing things their way, then it's likely that you're basically incompatible. For the relationship to work, you will both have to make some serious compromises. One will have to learn to back off a little and give the other space, and the other will need to learn to develop a language of intimacy and gestures of tenderness and affection so that both people get what they need. It will be hard work.

In a strong relationship, both people have the same or very similar values. Heed this warning: if you compromise your values for a relationship and ignore the resistance, the partnership will not last.

Career

If you value family but have a job in a highly competitive environment where you are expected to work long hours, do you think you would feel internal conflict? Could this be stressful for you? Some people might thrive in this environment, but they are likely to be the people who place career as a priority over family.

Health and Fitness

If you value health and fitness, how are you going to feel after a night out with friends that involved fatty food, alcohol and getting back home very, very late? You can avoid the guilt, disharmony, self-anger (and the hangover) the next day by avoiding the peer pressure and honouring your individual values.

Similarly, if you work long hours and can't get to the gym, then perhaps your job isn't really aligned with your values.

Hopefully these examples can help you to see that understanding your values can really assist you in avoiding situations that are going to cause you stress.

IDENTIFYING YOUR VALUES

Here is a list – circle the ones that resonate with you.

Abundance	Decisiveness	Health	Reflection
Acceptance	Delight	Helpfulness	Relaxation
Achievement	Dependability	Imagination	Reliability
Acknowledgement	Determination	Independence	Resilience
Adaptability	Devotion	Ingenuity	Respect
Adventure	Discipline	Insightfulness	Security
Affection	Discovery	Inspiration	Self-control
Ambition	Diversity	Intimacy	Self-reliant
Appreciation	Drive	Intuition	Selfless
Awareness	Duty	Joy	Sensitive
Balance	Empathy	Justice	Service
Belonging	Encouragement	Kindness	Significance
Bliss	Endurance	Leadership	Simplicity
Boldness	Energy	Liberation	Sincerity
Bravery	Enjoyment	Longevity	Solitude
Brilliance	Entertainment	Love	Spirituality
Calmness	Enthusiasm	Making a difference	Strength
Capability	Equality	Mastery	Structure
Care	Excellence	Mindfulness	Success
Certainty	Excitement	Motivation	Synergy
Challenge	Exploration	Open-mindedness	Teamwork
Charity	Fairness	Optimism	Trust
Compassion	Faith	Originality	Truth
Completion	Fame	Passion	Understanding
Composure	Family	Peace	Uniqueness
Concentration	Fearlessness	Persistence	Variety
Confidence	Fitness	Playfulness	Victory
Congruency	Flexibility	Pleasure	Vision
Connection	Flow	Popularity	Vitality
Consistency	Focus	Potency	Warmth
Contentment	Fortitude	Power	Wealth
Contribution	Freedom	Practicality	Winning
Cooperation	Fun	Presence	Wisdom
Courage	Gratitude	Privacy	Wittiness
Creativity	Growth	Proactive	Wonder
Curiosity	Happiness	Prosperity	Worthiness
Daring	Harmony	Punctuality	

Now, let's work out the ones you want to make a priority at this point in your life. What do you want to change? Focus on? Or Improve?

- Career
- Business
- Finances
- Wealth
- Friends
- Family
- Adventure
- Recreation
- Entertainment
- Health
- Fitness
- Love
- Personal development
- Professional development
- Spiritual development
- Physical environment

Once you have selected one, ask yourself what is important to you about it. For instance, if it's 'family', then analyse what you treasure about your close ones. It could be:

- Spending time together
- Eating dinner together
- Going to the movies together
- Going away on holidays together
- Being home in time for dinner
- Spending time shopping together
- Going out for coffee or lunch
- Having time to have deep and meaningful conversations

Now you try it.

Ask yourself: *What is important about* _____?

Write down what comes to mind – this will really help you to prioritise.

Note: when working out your values, it is important to know that your values are what's actually important to you right here and right now, and not what you would like to have or desire to be. For example, what's important to you about family? You may say, *'unconditional support'*. Is *'unconditional support'* something that you already own? Also, is it important to you or something that you aspire or desire to have?

Once you have completed your list, ask yourself: if I can only choose one, what will it be? Ask yourself this over and over again and you will develop a list – the first one you wrote will be the most important, with each one thereafter having decreasing value.

Then you will have a list of priorities, in order of preference.

My 6 top values are:

1.

2.

3.

4.

5.

6.

Now that you have your list of values, we are now going to add evidence that these are being met in your life.

Make a statement. Be clear and concise for each one. Your statement will be something along the lines of...

I will know that _____ (*my value*) is being met in my life when _____ I know it is being expressed when _____This latter part will help you to understand if your value is really being met in your life or if you just think it is. If you have to think back to the last time you felt *'joy'* or *'good health'*, then this is a sign that perhaps there are areas of your life you need to change so that your value is better expressed.

> *"Everyone's values are defined by what they will tolerate when it is done to others."* – **William Greider**

CIRCLE OF LIFE AND HAPPINESS

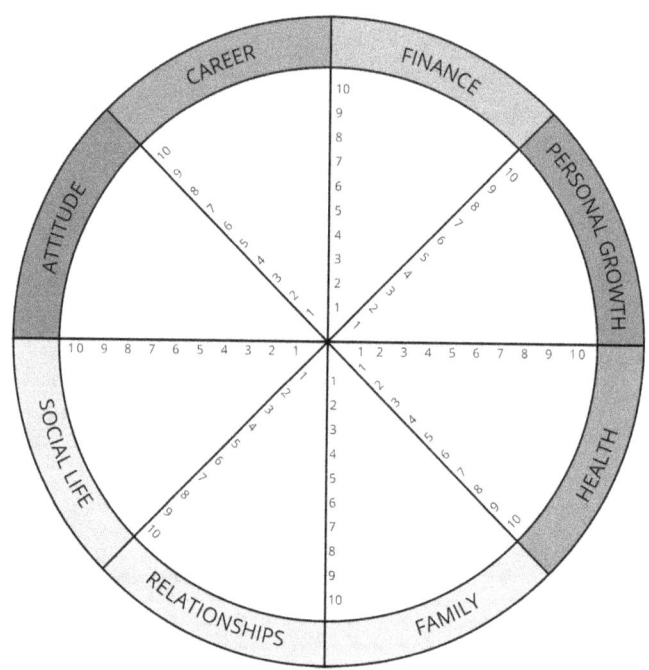

> *"There are only two ways to live your life. One is as though nothing is a miracle. The other is as though everything is a miracle."* –
> **Albert Einstein**

The circle of life is about creating balance, happiness and success in all areas of your life. This exercise splits your life into 8 key areas displayed around your circle of life. The purpose of your wheel of life is to identify how you are currently spending your time and how satisfied and happy you are in the different areas of your life.

Areas of your life examples are:

- Career
- Business
- Finances
- Wealth
- Friends
- Family
- Fun
- Adventure
- Recreation
- Entertainment
- Health
- Fitness
- Love
- Personal development
- Professional development
- Spiritual development
- Physical environment

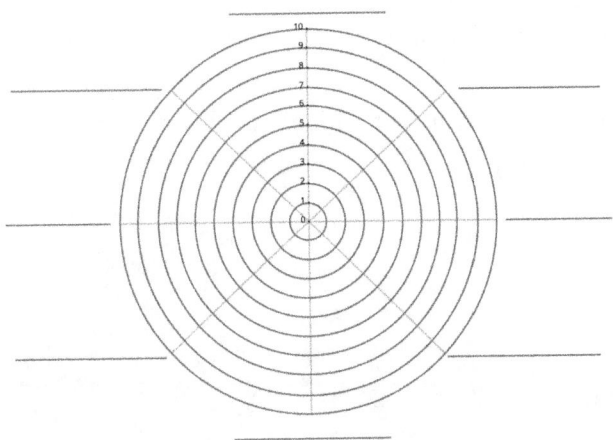

How to complete your life wheel – Instructions:

1. Identify 8 areas of your life that are most important to you.

You may choose to make them broad areas (i.e. **Health** may incorporate diet and exercise). Alternatively, you may choose more specific areas (i.e. **Diet** as a separate area).

Write your 8 chosen life areas around the wheel, on the lines at each wheel segment.

2. Examine one particular area. Spend time assessing how successful this particular aspect of your life feels right now. If you're humming along, then score highly in a ranking of 1–10 (10 is the 'highest'). If it's an area that needs some attention, then be honest, and score yourself accordingly. This is not a test. There is no right or wrong answer. This needs to be an honest assessment of where you are at. You will be surprised at the outcome.

Draw a cross at the score-point along the scale of that life area.

3. Now repeat the same process until you have assessed each life area.

4. At this point, join the dots... Draw a line from each cross you have drawn against each life area.

You may end up with a shape that looks a bit like this:

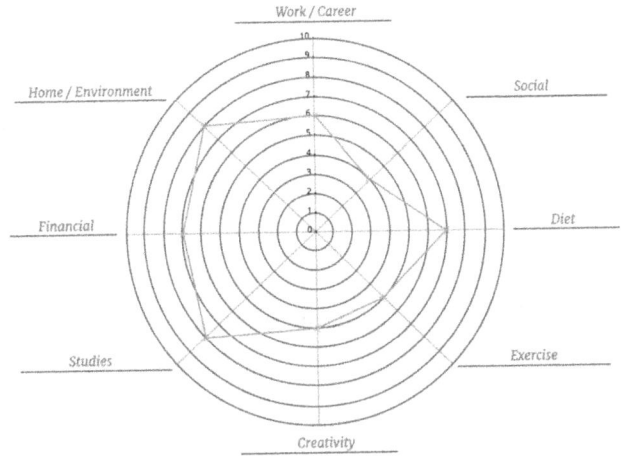

This will give you a picture representation of where you are right now, in relation to where you want to be for a number of important life areas.

Connect all the dots to see the shape of your wheel. If each of these areas contributes to your happiness, you can now add up your scores and give yourself a total out of 80 possible points to assess how satisfied you are with your life right now.

- Why does your *wheel of life* look this way?

___

- What would you like your *wheel of life* to look like?

___

- What areas of your *wheel of life* do you need to work on?

___

- What would you need to do to improve each area of your life?

- How will you make it happen?

- What areas of your *wheel of life* are you ready to make changes in?

Write a list and decide the priorities. Be sure to make a goal and a measure of success so you can celebrate appropriately when you get there!

CHAPTER 9
FINDING YOUR PASSION AND PURPOSE

"Being happy doesn't mean that everything is perfect. It means that you have decided to look beyond the imperfections."

MOMENTS OF HAPPINESS

Happiness requires you to get out of your head and jump into your heart which is precisely why it seems to elude some people.

Most of us spend our time thinking our way through life, but finding happiness requires us to connect with our heart space and do what we love.

How often do you meet someone who loves what they do? The local café owner, an artist working in a small collective, a librarian who gets to read and review new books. You see these individuals and think to yourself, '*Oh, he's or she's so lucky!*'.

Frankly, luck has nothing to do with it. These people are simply following their passion and have found their purpose. When that happens to you, you will never '*work*' a day again in your life because you will be so in love with what you're doing to earn a living.

Not many people love what they do. The reason for this is that we're conditioned by society and we '*think*' we need to get a job, earn a living to keep a roof over our heads and food on the table. Well, yes. We do need to do that, it's simply a practicality of living in our society, but that's not to say we can't enjoy ourselves while doing it. We fall into the trap of earning a living, rather than making a life because we're looking at this thing the wrong way around.

What you put out is what you will get back eventually – some call it karma. It is a universal law

We're thinking too much, instead of following our hearts and connecting with what makes us feel happy. We're often too attached to an external outcome. But, if we turn this around, and shift our attention inward and follow what makes us happy, we can solve the practicalities a different way.

It's also important to remember that our society can be quite materialistic. So, again, we become conditioned to working for the highest salary, seeking value in things, rather than experiences or people. We can fall into the trap of *'keeping up with the Jones'* because we think that is what's expected of us. In reality, we could do with accumulating less 'stuff' and spending more time doing what we love.

- Be honest, do you love what you do?
- Are you passionate about your job?
- Do you always give your best and do more than you are paid for?

GOING WITH THE FLOW

Do you recall a time when you were so involved with a project that you completely lost a sense of time? A time when you were so consumed by the very thing that you were doing that it was totally effortless? In fact, when you finished the job, you did not feel drained, but energetic? Empowered? Ready to go again?

When this happens, you have found your *flow*.

Flow is when you are totally focused and concentrating for a period of time. You feel at peace, serene and lost in the task, pouring your energy, your ideas and your efforts into what you're doing.

When you're in this state of mind, you're not conscious of your *'self'* and you're not aware of your physical body either. Many creative writers will tell you that's why they've ended up with shoulder problems or wrist problems. They get so into the moment of what they're doing, they forget to check in and make sure there's no stress or strain on the body while they're completing the task at hand.

Flow happens when we're fully engaged in the *'doing'* and our entire physical, emotional, mental and spiritual bodies are working as one. Each is completely absorbed in and dedicated to the activity of the moment.

How is it possible to achieve this kind of *flow* at work and in life?

The answer is simple. Follow your heart. Find your deepest, deepest desire and do what you love. Yes, there are practical considerations about bills to pay and mouths to feed, but there are numerous ways they can be accomplished in tandem. Start part time, study new skills, or join a group of like-minded souls.

Research shows that when you are engaged in doing something you're passionate about, your brain releases endorphins. An example would be oxytocin; the love hormone that amplifies optimism and positive emotions. All of these are not only critical for good mental health, but physical well-being too.

Happiness is our desire, our end result, whether we want a better relationship, more money or a good job – we are all seeking happiness.

Moreover, we can all benefit from having aspirations. But when we focus too hard on the outcome, we can often misdirect our energy and push it away. When we find flow, we channel energy calmly and continuously and harmoniously, without any angst or pressure.

It's also important to remember that we cannot change anything, unless we first accept it for what it is. Then, when we want to change something that's external, we need to change it from the inside first. When you want to change something external, something in your environment, then the *change* has to start internally.

When you surrender to that very thing that you want and have faith that it is yours, it will happen for you.

Your life is a perfect reflection of your beliefs.

WHAT WE FOCUS ON GROWS

The way that we look at things has an enormous bearing on our lives. All things, situations, people, experiences, they each have the meaning we attach to them. If we want to *change* anything in life, we must first see it for what it is, and then decide how we want it to be different. Only once we have done this can we can start to look at it in a different way and it will start to change.

For example, you might work with someone who you just don't *'click'* with. You might even say to yourself that this person *'drives you completely crazy'*. But if you can find just one thing to like about them, and then another and another, you can build a different picture. Your tolerance will increase. Maybe even one day you'll discover that you have something in common and start to develop a personal relationship with this person.

Non-verbal communication – *body language* – carries a lot of weight from the energy of our thoughts when we are relating to other people. Unconsciously, they will pick up on our signals too. When we change our attitude towards others, they respond accordingly.

Like attracts like – if you focus on the negative or a problem, you will have more problems or negativity in your life. But if you focus on the positive or on what is possible, then you will attract good things and more opportunities.

> *"There are no such things as problems, only 'possibilities' and 'opportunities'."*

HOW TO GET WHAT YOU WANT

> *"The soul never thinks without a picture."* – **Aristotle**

1. Be very clear about what it is that you want. Write it down and be very specific.
2. Create a *picture* in your mind – close your eyes and create the picture of that perfect relationship or that great job. Add more colours to your picture, make it bright and make it *big*.
3. Add *sound* to your picture. What noises characterise what you want?

4. Then, finally, add *feelings* to your picture. Where do you feel your emotions? What part of your body? Are the feelings intense or soft? Is there movement in your picture? What shapes are your feelings?
5. Once your picture or movie is complete, step into it. Now you are seeing through your own eyes as if you were really there. Tweak it if you need to, until it's exactly how you want it, and then absorb it so you can re-create it again at any time.
6. Now step out of your picture or movie and place your visualisation in a hot air balloon, watch it float into your future.

This is detachment of an outcome; you put your energy, heart and faith into knowing that it is going to be exactly what you ask for.

You have a choice

You can wallow in disappointment or anger, or sadness or you can focus on something that makes you feel happy, content, and peaceful. This doesn't mean that your sadness or grief or exasperation or dissatisfaction aren't valid feelings, it just means that you can, at any moment, start to help yourself shift that feeling to something more pleasant. Close your eyes and think of a happy moment. Once you connect with that happy moment, focus on your *heart* centre. How do you *feel*? Keep amplifying until you start to feel less negative, more positive!

It's that easy!

Remember, what you focus on grows.

Every day you have a choice as to what kind of day you are going to have. Will it be a *happy* day or will it be a miserable day for you? It all depends on your mindset. It helps to be completely *present* – to enjoy the beauty of your surroundings. Observe your favourite ornament, or a picture on your wall, the morning sun through the window, the chirping birds, and the taste of a hot cup of tea. Every day, the more you do this, you will increase your levels of happiness so that you can feel butterflies of joy in your heart and tummy.

Happiness is our birthright, it is our natural state of being – it is something that we choose and it is available to all of us.

That said, sometimes it's ok to go through the sorrow too – self-care is important and if you need to cry, cry. If you need to box it out at the gym or run 10 km, then do it. When you're ready to let go, you'll know.

But whatever happens, you have a choice. You decide how you feel.

> *"Don't cry because it's over, smile because it happened."*

FINDING YOUR PASSION AND PURPOSE

We are all here for a reason. And, we each have something to contribute to this human existence. We have a unique *gift, talent, super power*. Connecting with that gift or talent enables us to really live our lives to their fullest potential.

Finding your *passion* and *purpose* leads to success in your relationships and your career, because it connects you to your best self.

Passion is following your heart. *Purpose* keeps you on track and focused on your path.

Have you ever stopped to ask yourself:

- What is my purpose?
- Why am I here?
- What is my passion?
- How can I identify and uncover my passion?
- How do I live my purpose?

> *"When you see what you're here for, the world begins to mirror your purpose in a magical way. It's almost as if you suddenly find yourself*

on a stage in a play that was written expressly for you." – **Betty Sue Flowers**

Insights and reflection

'This is a great time to journal... Start to reflect, write out your answers so you can see the patterns that jump out at you.'

- As a child, what did you love to do the best?
- Was there anything you wanted to be or do?
- What did you most want to give to the world?

What about now – what do you love to do? This can be anything from painting, cooking or writing. What are you good at? Write a list. What are some of the things you have always wanted to do?

_____
_____
_____

Now, fill in the 2 columns below. One is called *creative* and the other is called *committed*, meaning that you were focused and determined. Write down all of the recent situations you can think of that have really required you to be creative. In the second column, write a list of times when you were totally committed to achieving a goal.

Creative	Committed

What are some of your best achievements in life that you are proud of? What are some of the most exciting times in your life? Choose a category and include them.

What was your greatest accomplishment? What are some things that come to mind that required a lot of persistence? Other questions you might include in this exercise are:

- What do you most enjoy about your work?
- What do you enjoy doing?
- What are your hobbies or interests?
- What do you most enjoy making and learning about?
- If money weren't a factor, what kind of work would you be doing?

Review your answers – can you see a pattern? What insights have you achieved from this exercise? What actions do you need to take to implement that very thing into your life right now?

For example, if writing was something that stood out from that exercise, you could tackle a little at a time. You could set an intention each day and work towards your passion. Start a blog or a journal. Take a course or join a writer's group. There are lots of ways you can take action towards fulfilling your passion.

Remember, once you take action (even in a small way) to include it in your life, then momentum will build.

IN PURSUIT OF YOUR PURPOSE

Why am I here?

Everything we achieve in life starts with passion. It is the very thing that fuels motivation, engagement and direction.

When you have a business idea, a great accomplishment or desire, passion is what shapes and defines your purpose in life or business.

Getting clear on 'why' you are here, your life direction and your *purpose* will help you develop, guide and create a successful strategy. In turn, this strategy will help you build a strong *vision* and *mission* for you to create a clear path. All you need to do is to follow your passion and lead with purpose to find your happiness.

Creating a mission statement will help you define your purpose and objectives; mission statements are powerful and bring clarity.

Creating a mission statement

A mission statement is a succinct statement that clearly describes the purpose of why you exist. It explains how your high-level, big dream will become a reality. A mission is something you share readily with others because it is practical and can be applied.

Why is it important to have a mission statement?

It's essential to have a mission because it gives you a clear focus on what you need to do. Even more, it gives everyone close to you an understanding of why you are here.

Define what you want to be, do and have.

- What do you want to be?

- What do you want to do?

- What do you want to have?

A one-sentence statement describing the reason you exist and for what purpose you do what you do.

This should be a practical, tangible tool you can use to make decisions about priorities, actions and responsibilities.

Your mission statement needs to:

- be clear and simple
- easily explained
- not confused with a vision statement
- be recognisably yours

When writing your *mission* statement, write it as if now, right in this moment you have already achieved it. Remember, the mind can't tell what is real and what is not real. As a result, if you make a statement as if already achieved, your reticular activating system, or your antennas that I spoke about in Chapter 3, will provide you with the evidence that, in turn, makes it real.

YOUR PERSONAL STRENGTHS

When it comes to your relationship or career, what are your personal qualities that make you a unique individual, setting you apart from everyone else? If you are not sure or this is a blind spot for you, ask your friends and family to help you.

What do you consider your strongest character traits?

_____
_____
_____

More than anything, what sets you apart as a unique individual?

_____
_____
_____

> *Strength and growth come only through continuous effort and struggle."* – **Napoleon Hill**

IDENTIFYING YOUR 10 TOP TALENTS

Some people find it hard to identify their own strengths and talents, either because they are not aware of them or underestimate their importance. Our greatest potential for personal growth lies within our talents and strengths. Likewise, feel free to ask friends and family for feedback to help with this task. They're the ones who know you well.

_____
_____
_____
_____
_____

Now you can begin to write your first draft. You might have many drafts of your mission statement before you feel like you can truly be aligned with it. It needs to represent the very best version of you. It must light you up with excitement. It must give you motivation, direction and purpose. But, above all, it must continue to inspire you every time you read it.

A good test is to read it out loud. Stumbles and mental blocks can be signs of resistance. Be aware of the feeling deep inside you. If it feels good, go for it. If you sense it's not right, go back to the keyboard!

Vision statement

Creating a personal vision statement takes time because you need to reflect deeply upon your desires and understand wholeheartedly what you want to become or what you want to achieve.

Like your *Mission statement*, it needs to be one single, simple statement.

When you create your vision, choose the right frame of mind and the right setting. You need quiet, and no distractions. Ask yourself the following questions:

- What kind of legacy are you leaving to the world?

  _____

- What would you like to be known for?

  _____

- What is the motivation for my vision?

  _____

- How does my vision help others?

  _____

- How am I going to commit to my vision?

- MISSION

- VISION

Once you have articulated your *Mission* and your *Vision*, you can get on with achieving them!

> "*I dream, I test my dreams against my beliefs, I dare to take risks and I execute my vision to make those dreams come true.*" – **Walt Disney**

CHAPTER 10
COMMUNICATION IS LIKE OXYGEN

'A good relationship starts with good communication.'

SUCCESSFUL COMMUNICATION AND RELATIONSHIPS

When we consider successful relationships between people, we often think about what these people might have in common. A few examples might be: shared interests, ideas, aspirations, the feelings (love, respect and trust) between them, the history (how long they have known each other) or the energy or attraction that draws them together.

Often, we believe that this magic cocktail of ingredients is enough to keep relationships going. But the truth is: it's not.

Successful, authentic relationships are built on mutual communication. These other elements play a part, but they are each determined, shaped, enhanced and perpetuated by our ability to communicate with each other. In the same way, these components can be damaged by our communication, or lack of communication, in relationships too.

Words can be powerful – they have the ability to inspire or injure! But, of course, communication is more than just *what* we say.

Here's a staggering fact about the way we communicate.

At any given moment in time, we are bombarded with information coming into our brain via our 5 senses at the speed of 2 million bits-per-second.

Generally speaking, we capture 126 bits of this information.

The math looks like this:

$$2,000,000 - 126 = 1,999,874$$
$$126 / 1,999,874 = 0.000063$$

Out of 2 million parcels of information, we *do not receive* 1,999,874.

Almost <u>all</u> of it.

Also, if we're in a poor state of mind, tired, stressed, not focused, preoccupied or busy multi-tasking, then we receive even less information.

So, given that we're missing *most* of the bits of information that are sent our way, is it *any wonder* we're suffering from a lack of communication in our relationships?

The very essence of successful communication is response.

Basically, when you are communicating with someone, you have to consider how the other person is interpreting the data that's coming from you. Even though what you're saying makes complete sense to you, the person you're talking to has their own interruptions. They could be external noise, possible language barriers, fatigue or maybe just other stuff on their mind while you're talking. These factors impact the amount of information they receive. They also impact how they process the information coming from you.

To be better partners, friends, mothers, fathers, employees, siblings and citizens, we all need to take greater responsibility for our communication – our relationships will immediately benefit. It's also important to remember that non-verbal communication, such as body language and facial expressions, are much stronger than what we say and how we say it.

If the receiver does not understand what you are trying to say, it is sensible to keep trying to get your point across until they do. In return, when someone is talking to you, active listening will help you to master great communication skills. We're all guilty of *hearing* what people say, but not really *listening to what they mean*. Providing feedback is a good way to demonstrate what you've heard; active listening means being truly present.

Remember:

- We listen to obtain information
- We listen to understand
- We listen for enjoyment

- We listen to learn

Here are some interesting facts:

- We listen to people at a rate of 125–250 words per minute, but we think at around 1,000 to 3,000 words per minute.

- When we process what someone is telling us, we get 55% of the information from the speaker's facial expressions and body language, 38% from the tone of voice and how the message is said and only 7% from the actual words that are spoken.

- In terms of memory – words go into the short-term memory bank and images go into the long-term memory bank. For this reason, images are often more successful at communicating than words are. For example, if you want to explain a circle to someone, it is easier to draw it than to describe it. Afterwards, your audience will immediately understand it.

It's also true that:

- Listening does not come naturally to most people.
- In conversation, we often jump in and give our point of view as soon as there's a pause.
- We sometimes ignore what's being said to us because we're listening to our own internal frequency – the dialogue inside our heads.
- We sometimes pretend to hear what people are saying just to appear polite, even though we are not particularly interested in the topic.
- We sometimes have selective hearing and ignore what we don't want to hear.

"One of the greatest gifts we can give is to make people feel seen, heard and recognised as the miracle they truly are." – **Emmanuel**

More often than not, emotions get in the way of clear, genuine communication. One way of dealing with emotions is to have a conversation with them. Imagine your fear, anger, sadness or some other negative emotion sitting in a chair in front of you. Ask questions like:

- Why are you here?
- What do you want me to do?
- How can I learn from you?

You might be surprised by your responses. Emotions give us powerful insight into ourselves. When we ignore them, they become stronger and more powerful – desperate for our attention. When we acknowledge them as they arise and give them due consideration, they can be valuable indicators of various aspects of our lives.

When you have finished your little chat, you can ask your emotion to go. Politely, of course, so you can open yourself up to new experiences.

EMPATHY

Empathy is being able to see the other side, to see another person's point of view.

While empathy and emotional intelligence are attributes we have long applied to our personal relationships, in recent times there has been a lot of research published about the importance of empathy and emotional intelligence (EQ) in business relationships too. If you are in a position of leadership, empathy is a key skill for understanding your people – what motivates and inspires them. It also helps to improve relationships with customers and clients, because empathetic people are able to communicate well and can influence others which help to build engagement.

What is empathy?

- Seeing with the eyes of another
- Listening with the ears of another
- Feeling with the heart of another
- Understanding the feelings and situations of another
- Being sensitive and aware of another
- Lending a hand when you see another in need

While empathy comes naturally to some people, others have to work at it. If you fall into the latter group, don't worry, it can be developed.

Here is how you can practice and express empathy.

Be curious

Curiosity expands your empathy. When you talk to people outside your usual social circle, encountering lives and worldviews are very different from your own. You're opening up your own knowledge of the world.

Being curious also means asking questions. Have a genuine interest in other people and you'll be surprised and delighted at what you encounter.

Listen carefully

Empathetic listening can only be done when you are truly present. This implies listening completely with your eyes, ears and heart, allowing others to have deep and meaningful conversations with you by giving them the space to do so. Stay focused on the *here* and *now*. Leave your own emotions at the door and just listen, without judgement or reaction. Pay attention to the non-verbal signs.

Show vulnerability

Far from what we might be brought up to believe, vulnerability is strength and not a sign of weakness. It takes courage to be vulnerable – remove your mask and reveal your feelings. Be open and honest and you will reap the rewards of authentic communication.

How are you communicating to yourself?

Of course, the way we interact with others takes up a large percentage of our energy and thought processes, but we also spend a lot of time talking to ourselves.

We all have that little voice inside our heads. It's important that we take control.

When you are fully present in your life, you're able to catch yourself saying those silly, negative thoughts. Then you can edit your communication and start to tell yourself a different story.

Remember: you are in charge of your life. When you nurture yourself and love yourself, you will thrive!

Celebrate uniqueness

We all put labels on people. To be fair, sometimes it helps to be able to distinguish our *tribe* from another. But these *generalisations* that we apply to people are based primarily on exterior cues, like the clothes they wear, the music they listen to and where they live. Making assumptions this way has a place, sometimes, but if we do it often, it distracts us from finding out who people really are... We miss out because we don't explore people's uniqueness.

Being empathetic takes effort. Some days it is hard to find the motivation to really *meet* someone at level that is more than *skin deep*. But when you do, you will find yourself being able to imagine walking around in their shoes for a little while. Then you can better understand other's thought processes, motivations and perspectives. This makes the world a much more intriguing place!

Without a doubt, empathy is rewarding. Sharing your life with others and showing them how different you are can bring great personal satisfaction. Offering to learn their differences too, by trying to see what they see, hear what they hear, feel what they feel might help you understand why they do what they do.

> *"I think we all have empathy. We may not have enough courage to display it."* – **Maya Angelou**

DO WE SPEAK THE SAME LANGUAGE?

The way we communicate is often unconscious. It's something hard-wired into our brains and we don't tend to give it much thought. Imagine how powerfully we could communicate if we took extra care with the words we used?

We've talked about the power that active listening can bring to communication, what about the way in which we speak – the phrases, the tone, the body language – and the impact these might have on our ability to build a meaningful connection with others. Let's explore our opportunities for boosting communication.

INTERNAL REPRESENTATION TEST

We each have an Internal Representation Systems. When we tap into them, we can harness their power and use them to assist us to communicate with each other. The Internal Representation Systems (IRS) is made up of our 5 key senses. These senses are the ways in which we represent, code, store and give meaning to the way that we view the world and interact in the world.

As such, the IRS has a huge influence over the way we communicate – in particular our preferences for receiving information, as well as the way we give information out. You can find out more about your own Internal Representational Systems by taking this short test.

Part 1

For each of the following statements, please place a number next to every phrase. Use the following system to indicate your preference:

4 = closest to describing you

3 = next best description

2 = next best

1 = least descriptive of you

For the first part of this exercise, do not pay attention to the capital letters in bold at the end of each statement option. You will only need them in the second part.

1. I make important decisions based on:

___ Gut level feelings **(K)**

___ Which way sounds the best **(A)**

___ What looks best to me **(V)**

___ Precise review and study of the issue **(AD)**

2. During an argument I am most likely to be influenced by:

___ The other person's tone of voice **(A)**

___ Whether or not I can see the other person's point of view **(V)**

___ The logic of the other person's argument **(AD)**

___ Whether or not I am in touch with the other person's true feelings **(K)**

3. I most easily communicate what is going on with me by:

___ The way I dress and look **(V)**

___ The feelings I share **(K)**

___ The words I choose **(AD)**

___ My tone of voice **(A)**

4. It is easiest for me to:

___ Find the ideal volume and tuning on a stereo system **(A)**

___ Select the most intellectually relevant point in an interesting subject **(AD)**

___ Select the most comfortable furniture **(K)**

___ Select rich, attractive colour combinations **(V)**

5. I am very:

___ Attuned to the sounds of my surroundings **(A)**

___ Adept at making sense of new facts and data **(AD)**

___ Sensitive to the way articles of clothing feel on my body **(K)**

___ Receptive to colours and to the way a room looks **(V)**

Part 2

Write down the numbers associated with each letter. There are 5 entries for each letter, which correspond to the 5 statements you rated options for.

For example, if you rated the first option for the first statement with 4 (meaning it is the closest to describing you), you would write the number '4' under the letter 'K' for the 1st row of the table below. If you rated the second option for the first statement with 3, you would place a '3' under 'A', and so on.

After you write down the number for each letter and statement, add them to see where you got the greatest amounts.

	V	A	K	Ad
1.				
2.				
3.				
4.				
5.				
Total				

Part 3

Interpreting your score

Once you have worked out your scores, this is your most common or evident internal representation system. It's okay if you have close numbers or even identical numbers; there is always one more leading than another, depending on your environment.

What are the different internal representational systems?

Visual (V) – People who are *'visual'* are better at memorising information when they can imagine. If you can truly *'paint them a picture with words'* by being descriptive, using analogies or even photos, diagrams and other visual aids, then you will strengthen the messages that you are sending to them. These people often have trouble remembering and are bored or turned off by long verbal instructions. This can lead to their mind wandering and they won't hear a word you've said. They are very interested in how things *'look'*.

Auditory (A) – Typically, people who are *'auditory'* are easily distracted by noise. If you have something really important to say to someone who falls into this category, take them somewhere quiet. Turn the radio and the TV off! They can repeat things back to you, and they learn easily by listening. They generally like music and talking on the phone. Tone of voice and word choice can be important.

Kinaesthetic (K) – Kinaesthetic individuals often talk slow and breathy. They respond to physical rewards and touching. They memorise concepts by *'acting out'* or *'walking through'* the idea – they need to be *'going through the motions'* to understand and really engage. They will be interested in what *'feels right'* or gives them a gut feeling.

Auditory Digital (Ad) – They spend a fair amount of time talking to themselves. They memorise by steps, procedures and sequences. They will want to know that the program makes sense. They can also sometimes exhibit characteristics of other representational systems like auditory and kinaesthetic.

HOW CAN YOU USE INTERNAL REPRESENTATIONAL SYSTEMS?

Your preferences (determined by your scores) will indicate how you are likely to communicate to others. The reason is that we tend to treat others the way we want to be treated and we talk to others using the same language we use when we talk to ourselves. However, being truly effective in communicating with others means moving away from our own natural preferences. We should work to understand other people's preferences so that we can communicate much more effectively. Step out of your communication style into their communication style and watch the magic. There is an instant connection; a fast way to build rapport.

Obviously, you can't put everyone you know or meet through the test! Nevertheless, the following list of words can help you to determine what Internal Representation System a person might have.

Visual	**Auditory**	**Kinaesthetic**	**Auditory Digital**
See	Hear	Feel	Abstract
Look	Listen	Touch	Idea
View	Sounds	Grasp	Understand
Appear	Music	Get hold of	Information
Show	Harmonise	Slip through	Process
Dawn	Tune in/out	Catch on	Learn
Reveal	Be all ears	Tap into	Think
Envision	Rings a bell	Make contact	Thought
Illuminate	Silence	Throw out	Know
Imagine	Be heard	Turn around	Data
Clear	Resonate	Hard	Facts
Foggy	Deaf	Unfeeling	Concept
Focused	Dissonance	Concrete	Program
Hazy	Question	Scrape	System
Crystal	Unhearing	Get a handle on	Analyse
Picture	Grating	Solid	Statistics

In a nutshell, if you can spot these words in conversations regularly, then you can approach your communication using tools that appeal to the Internal Representational System of the person you're talking to.

Evidently, this is only effective one-on-one, but it's useful to remember. It comes in handy if you often seem to be having *'crossed wires'* with someone, or you have something critical that you want them to know or learn, to boost your communication skills in a way that appeals directly to them, and which guarantees they will comprehend more of what you're saying.

THE CRAFT OF COMMUNICATION

Finding common ground really helps us to master the art of communication. The hierarchy of ideas takes this concept one step further, suggesting that we can master the art of communication by controlling the flow of conversation or ideas from abstract to specific and vice versa.

The key here is to know that in any interaction, the person who controls the level of abstraction or specificity will end up controlling and influencing the communication.

Think about this for a moment: have you ever had a conversation with someone and you are listening to him or her, waiting for more details?

Consider the statement below:

> *Something is wrong with our relationship...*

After looking at the statement, I am sure you are wondering what's actually wrong with the relationship. Can you see how many things can go wrong with a relationship?

The opposite can also happen, when someone is talking about something so specific that we have absolutely no idea what the conversation is all about.

Understanding how we can move someone through the hierarchy of ideas is a very effective and empowering tool.

Now, stay with the topic, it does get a little bit complicated, but it's nothing you can't handle and this really is worth knowing. It is a great tool for reaching a better understanding of our conversations and avoiding potential conflict! Consider the diagram below:

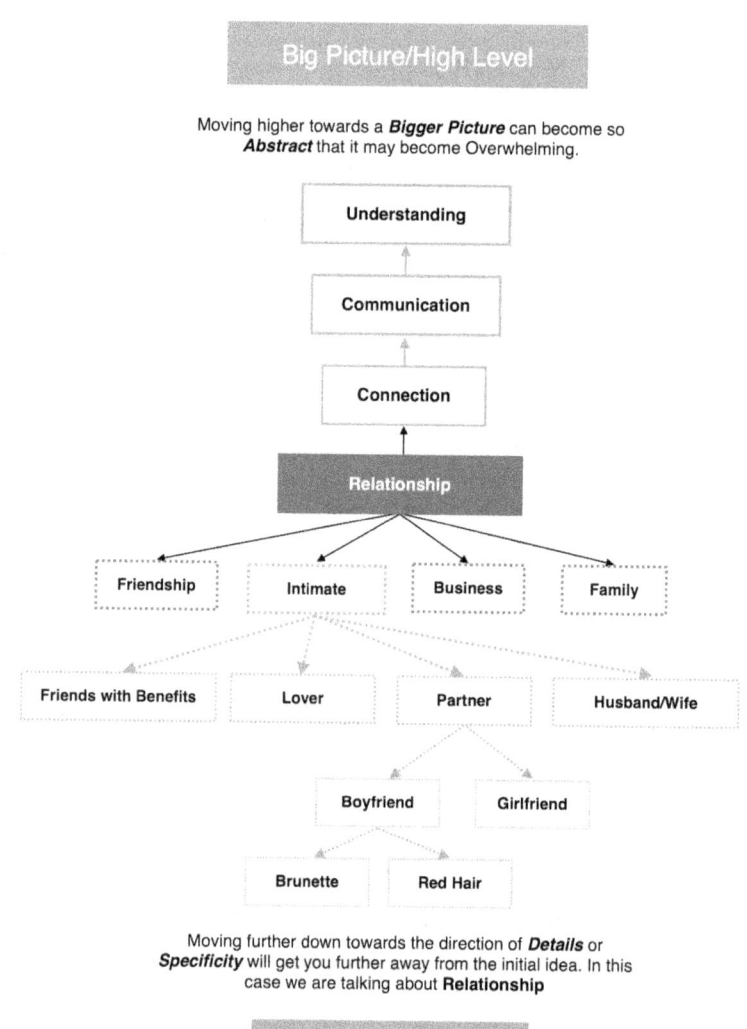

As you can see in the centre of the diagram, we are going to look at the idea of **Relationship**.

Let's say we want to have a conversation about *Relationship*. We actually have 2 directions that we can take the conversation to:

- We can talk about the intention or purpose of a Relationship, meaning we are moving to a bigger picture or topic.
- We can talk about different kinds or types of Relationships, which means we are moving into a more specific concept or idea.

On the other hand, imagine we want to start a conversation about *relationship* and we start talking about hair colour. Do you think the other person would know right away that you are talking about *relationship*? No possible way! The main reason is because we are talking about something way too specific.

The same will happen if you start talking about the importance of **Understanding**, the first element in our diagram. As you can see, *understanding* is a bigger concept and encompasses so many other ideas within it.

You may be wondering: how do I move the conversation from *Abstract* to *Specific* and vice versa? Very simple!

THE CONCEPT OF 'CHUNKING'

There are some new terms to come to grips with in this section: *Chunking Up*, *Chunking Down* and *Lateral Chunking*.

Chunking Up

We *'chunk up'* to come to an agreement and understanding. We also chunk up to separate intention from behaviour by asking a series of questions. These are extremely helpful when you want to move your ideas and concepts towards a bigger picture or resolution. This does not mean that you need to ask all of these questions to reach the desired level of abstraction (or even a bigger chunk). Depending on the context or content, the following may apply:

- What is this an example of?
- For what purpose?
- What is your intention?
- What will that do for you?

Let's use one example out of each of them.

Example – 2 people are planning a holiday. One of them really wants to go to Europe, while the other one only wants to go to Venice. We can begin by looking at the person wanting to go to Venice and ask ourselves the question: what's Venice an example of? Answer: a city in Italy! Easy, right? What's Italy an example of? A city in Europe. Bingo! We are on agreement now, can you see it! The key here is to bring the 2 parties or points of view into the same level or *'chunk-size'*. In this example, we now have the 2 parties looking and talking about Europe.

Purpose – Going back to our relationship example and our diagram; if you look, you can see that we have *Relationship* by itself in the middle. Let's ask ourselves the question: what's the purpose of a relationship? You may think: Connection. Ask yourself that same question once more: connection, for what purpose? Communication. Have you noticed that we are moving up to a bigger concept or idea? Can you feel that agreement is more achievable at this level compared to lower and more specific information?

Intention – We can continue with the same idea (i.e. communication) and ask ourselves: what's the intention of communication? Understanding, would be the next answer.

Do for you – Since now you understand that each of these questions creates upward movement; we can now quickly look at the last question on the list and apply it to communication. You can ask yourself: communication, what would that do for me? Your potential answer: it will help me reach understanding. See how we have gone up again?

The whole idea is to be clear with each question that will facilitate the upward or chunking up movement to help you reach your desired outcome.

Chunking up will open your possibilities and opportunities in any interaction or situation, no matter how difficult they may seem to be.

Chunking Down

We *'chunk down'* to understand details and distinctions. We also chunk down to maintain agreement for an action by asking the questions below:

- What are examples of this?
- What specifically?
- Whom specifically?

We'll set examples for each question using the same *Relationship* concept from our diagram.

Examples – what are examples of a *Relationship*? You may answer: Family, Business, Intimate or Friendship; very easy, right?

What – Moving on to the second question: what specifically is an intimate relationship? You will probably answer: partner. Excellent!

Whom – Last question! Looking at partner: whom specifically? Boyfriend or Girlfriend?

Have you noticed how we have moved from *Relationship* all the way down to *Boyfriend* or *Girlfriend*?

Lateral Chunking

When we *'lateral chunk'*, typically we're doing so to access other examples. The question to get another example of a chunk is:

- What is another example of _____?

In order to make this very easy for you, you should first do a quick Chunk-Up and the question above will automatically chunk the concept right back to the initial level. Let's do a fast and simple example for this:

> *We are at a party and someone keeps talking about Paris. We have never been to Paris, but we want to be part of the conversation and we have only visited Bordeaux and Lyon. Quietly, we can ask ourselves: what is Paris an example of? A city in France! Let's do the lateral chunk now: what is another example of a city in France? We have 2 options now (Bordeaux or Lyon). We can now join the conversation without going off-topic.*

Can you see how we went up and right back down when we did the lateral chunk?

Interestingly, the mind actually *'chunks up'* intuitively to find connections and relationships, and then *'chunks back down'* to relate to the current situation we find ourselves in. So, we already know how to do this.

However, when we actually do it *mindfully*, our ability to relate with others can be very powerful.

For instance, you and your partner are considering buying a new car. Your partner has his heart set on a BMW and you have your heart set on a SUV. Both of you believe that what you want is the best option and the conversation is getting heated.

The reason you're on the brink of an argument in this situation is that you're both too caught up in the specifics of the car – *chunked down* – and you can't see eye-to-eye, because what you're both focused on is very different and *very 'chunked down'* – specific.

In this situation, if you changed direction and started *'chunking up'*, you would soon get to the purpose or intention behind your desire for a new car and the conversation changes tack. Argument avoided!

When 2 people are in conflict, they are normally chunking down with their conversation as well as their thinking – getting bogged in the specifics of the detail. When you *'chunk up'*, the conversation will eventually get to some common ground and then you're out of *'argument territory'* and you can have a productive discussion.

'Chunking up' might go something like this:

Thomas	Addison
I want to lose 20 kilos	What's the purpose of losing 20 kilos? I think you look fantastic.
To feel good	What would that do for you?
Improve my health	What's the intention of being healthy?
Longevity	Oh, it's fantastic you want to be around me for longer!

In the example above, you can see that, at the beginning of it, there was a little bit of resistance from your partner's side in terms of losing the 20 kilos. As Addison moved the conversation to a higher level of abstraction (or bigger chunk), they finally reached a point where she knew that it was a win-win situation for the 2 of them!

Chunking up is a fun tool to use when you are:

- Solving problems in communication
- Trying to gain agreement
- Negotiating
- Exploring thoughts and ideas for new projects
- Finding common ground

CHAPTER 11
RAPPORT IS LIKE A DANCE

'The inspiration and genius you seek are already within you.'

BUILDING RAPPORT AND EFFECTIVE COMMUNICATION

Rapport is the harmony between 2 people who understand each other's feelings and ideas and communicate well.

Have you ever noticed how conversations just flow when people are in rapport? Their bodies are in sync, their words match each other and their energies are intertwined. It is magical to observe.

Just watch! The next time you are out for dinner or out for a drink, watch a couple and see how they pick up their glass in unison, matching each other's body language and speaking style. It is like a dance. The dance of rapport is what we do naturally when we are with someone we feel connected to.

Rapport is that amicable 2-way connection – the solid foundation of any relationship. It doesn't just *'happen'*. It occurs between people who have mutual understanding, similar values and synergistic drives.

While it is easier to build rapport to someone with similar values and life experiences to your own, those are not necessarily mandatory. People of all ages, backgrounds, colours and creeds can have great rapport, provided they first make an effort to really see each other and to accept each other for who they are. It's possible to do this when you:

- Take a genuine interest in what someone has to say
- Find out about the person; their background, likes and dislikes
- Explore interests and hobbies and aim to find some *'common ground'*
- Use the key words we've discussed to create a connection
- Observe body language and mirror it
- Mirror their breath

If you stay focused, actively listening and using other practical tools that will enhance your communication skills, then you will start to build rapport with the people that you meet.

One bit of advice, don't make it too obvious or you will end up with a slap across the head – sort of speaking.

Trust and business

There's no denying that rapport is easier to forge in personal relationships. It is more challenging to forge in business relationships where there are often more *'boundaries'* and *'formalities'* placed on the way we communicate. Generally, we spend less time with the people we are in business with, all of which can hinder our ability to build rapport. But it's not completely impossible to do.

Here are some strategies to try in your professional relationships:

- Greet customers and people by their name
- Get good at small talk; ask questions
- Pay attention to the answers
- Be approachable and smile
- Speak in their language and use their key words to create connection
- Listen with your eyes, ears and heart

No rapport

Most of us have experienced, at one time or another, a situation where we just have no rapport with the person we are communicating with.

It can be unbearably uncomfortable.

Sometimes, rapport can be fragile too and even though it exists, a simple word can destroy it. From that point, it's hard to rebuild.

But have you ever noticed that people who have great rapport tend to sort of *'match'* each other? People who don't have good rapport tend to mismatch. A good tip for those times when you're trying to build rapport is to *'mimic'* the person you're trying to connect with. You can do this by matching and mirroring body language, facial expression, tone and pitch. Children are naturally great at this.

Agree to disagree

To build rapport, you don't have to like or even agree with the other person's view of the world. Nevertheless, if you want to build rapport, you have to make a really big attempt at understanding it.

When you are in rapport with someone, you can completely disagree with them and still respectfully relate with each other. This comes down to accepting people for the unique individuals that they are.

Non-verbal communication

We're taught from an early age that communication is much more than the words we speak. There is a myriad of non-verbal ways to communicate that we should all be well-aware of.

Robert Birdwhistle, who researched communication in the 1970s, studied how face-to-face communication was received and responded to. His work suggests that your impact depends on 3 factors: how you *look*, how you *sound* and what you *say*.

According to Birdwhistle, 55% of communication is body language (physiology) – posture, gestures, facial expressions, blinking and breathing.

38% is the quality of the voice (tonality) tone, speed, quality and volume.

Only 7% is the actual words spoken, predicates, key words, and common experiences, content chunks.

Body language refers to our non-verbal communications – *facial expressions* and *body movements*. Basically, what we don't say can still convey volumes of information. These too all help us to build rapport.

THE 4 INDICATORS OF RAPPORT

These indicators will help you to know when you have established rapport. You will already be familiar with these terms, as they are the same ones used for our Internal Representation Systems exercise that we completed a few pages before.

You might experience more than one of these at any one time:

Kinaesthetic – Internal feeling or butterflies.

Visual – Colour shift. There might be a change in colour for both people, usually the neck. You may feel it yourself internally or notice it in the other person from light to dark.

Auditory – They may say something to indicate that you are in rapport. For example – *Do I know you?* Or – *have we met before?* Or – *I feel like we have known each other for years.*

Auditory Digital – Leading is a state of responsiveness, indicating that both people are responding to each other. One highly positive indicator is when the other person begins to follow you. You can test this by lifting your glass for a drink or sitting forward in your chair.

RAPPORT AND TRUST

If you have rapport with someone, do you have trust?

No, not necessarily. Trust is fragile, and it is usually earned rather than given away freely. This means that you will only get it in relationships where you've known each other for a little while. In other words, at least enough time to get to know each other, and share some experiences so you can figure out whether or not you've met someone you want to trust.

There are different levels of trust, expressed through non-verbal communication:

- Trust instantly
- Earn trust
- Or don't trust at all

The issue in this day and age is that we do everything at double-speed! We have moved communication online, via text or over the phone and not all that often in person.

This really makes it difficult to get to know someone's authentic self. It also makes opportunities to learn about each other harder to find. When we're meeting and getting to know people via screens, we are just reading words and looking at pictures. We are unable to take into account any of the other vital communication clues such as tone of voice, facial expression and body language. In many cases, this is why relationships fall apart because, if we're honest, we are rushed. On the other hand, we might not have taken the appropriate time or made the effort to truly get to know each other.

EMOTIONAL BANK ACCOUNT

Stephen Covey, in *'The 7 Habits of Highly Effective People'*, talks about the Emotional Bank Account, which is an account of trust instead of money. It's an account based on how safe we feel with another person. By making deposits, we create and build on positive moments with our partner. Emotional savings will serve as a cushion when times get tough.

Major Deposits	Major Withdrawals
Understanding the individual	Belittling the individual
Attending to little things	Condemning or judging them
Keeping commitments	Getting angry or lashing out
Clarifying expectations	Criticising
Showing personal integrity	Acting deceptively
Forgiving	Taking advantage of the individual
Kindnesses, courtesies	Breaking promises
Loyalty to the absent	Acts of unkindness, discourtesies
Acknowledgement	Violating expectations
Being open to feedback	Disloyalty to the absent – gossip, rumours

I encourage you to do regular deposits into your emotional bank account with all the important people you have in your life. Keep your balance high.

Restoring trust with those around you can be very rewarding but also an enormously positive adventure.

Take the time to do your own *'audit'* of your relationship with a friend or partner. See what you can come up with from your experiences with each other over the past couple of weeks.

Major Deposits	Major Withdrawals

What about you?

'Personal bank accounts are just as significant.'

As much as it is important to understand and get insight into your emotional bank account with other people, what about *you*? This is a fundamental part of self-care. The analogy is simple – too many withdrawals without topping up the funds lead to bankruptcy. Don't let it happen to you. You cannot possibly be your very best self unless you take time to look after *you*.

- What do you do that you love?

- How much do you love *you*? *From 1 (not very much) to 10 (heaps)!*

- Do you feel confident about *you* and what you do?

- How much time do you spend with *you*, improving yourself?

- Do you follow your passions or hobbies?

- How often do you exercise?

- Do you take care of your health? *From 1 (not very much) to 10 (heaps)!*

- What is your personal brand? Do you dress to impress?

- How often do you learn new things to grow?

- What are your dreams?

- Do you compromise your values?

- Do you keep your promises to you?

- Are your thoughts positive about you?

When you love yourself and when you keep promises to yourself, you honour *you*. Always look at how you can make deposits into your personal account every day!

Examples below are of what your personal emotional account may look like.

Major Deposits	Major Withdrawals
Keep promises to yourself	Break personal promises
Do small acts of kindness	Keep to yourself and be selfish
Be gentle with yourself	Think negatively about yourself
Be honest and stand in your truth	Be dishonest and lie
Reward your achievements	Burn out and wear yourself out
Use your strengths and tap into your talents	Ignore your talents and focus only on your weaknesses
Renew yourself	Stay stuck and be a victim of life

Perhaps conduct your own audit here. What transactions have you made over the past 2 weeks?

Major Deposits	Major Withdrawals

CHAPTER 12
ACCOUNTABILITY BREEDS RESPONSIBILITY

'You are one decision away from a totally different life.'

SELF-RESPONSIBILITY AND ACCOUNTABILITY

No room for excuses!

Make it happen, own it and find a solution!

Oh, what an empowering position to be in – don't you think?

When you're fully accountable for your actions, you find out what you're really capable of. You make mistakes, you own those mistakes and you learn from them.

Accountability builds responsibility, trust and respect – these are big words in anyone's language.

When you are personally accountable, you take ownership of your actions and choices – then your accountability extends beyond your own actions. You don't blame others when things go wrong. Instead, you go out of your way to make things right. It's also a fact that those individuals who take personal accountability have better social interactions with others because their accountability builds *trust* and *respect*.

An individual who is personally accountable will be considered dependable, responsible and trustworthy. What follows is that friends and family members will go the *'extra mile'*, unconditionally too, just because they have an appreciation for your transparency, accountability and responsibility.

Behaviour breed's responsibility. This refers to the manner in which one behaves; the action or reactions of a person to an external or internal stimulation. A perfect example is: *if looks could kill*. What kind of behaviour will be a result from those emotions or displaying negative behaviours?

Accountability is not something that is automatic or comes naturally for some people. But it can become an acquired skill. We all make mistakes. When we own up to them, are present and accountable, we are standing in our own truth. This is far easier than blaming others.

Blaming others gives our power away. When we *'own'* it, we have the power to work with it. Learning how to fix things and resolve situations and problems is a much more powerful and rewarding frame of mind.

Tips to become more accountable:

- **Don't say *yes* to everything.** Manage your time and resources wisely. Things will fall through the cracks if you overcommit.

- **Watch out for procrastination.** This is a sign that you are avoiding dealing with the problem. As soon as you find yourself procrastinating, stop and check in with your priorities. It's likely that you'll find that the very thing you're procrastinating about is the exact thing you should be focused on.

- **Ask for feedback.** 3 questions I love to ask that give me insight into my blind spots are:

o What am I doing right?
o What opportunities for improvement do you see for me?
o *What can I do differently?*

If we want others to do the same, then we just need to be a role model for this behaviour and give others a good example to follow. The key attributes here are all habits that can be learned. All it takes is a little courage, a little effort and a little understanding.

CAUSE AND EFFECT APPLIED

What is Cause and Effect?

Cause is the reason something happens. The effect is the thing that happens as a result of the cause, or when one event causes another to happen. The cause is *why* it happens. The effect is *what* happens.

How to put it into practice

Firstly, you have to identify and write down the exact problem. Once you have the problem, use the chart below to identify which side of the problem you have in front of you. Is it the *'what'* of the problem? If it is, put it into the Effect side of the column. Is it a *'why'* of the problem, the reason it happened? Then write it in the Cause side of the column.

The exercise here is to sort out all your problems by being in power or control of each situation. The best way to describe it is asking yourself why you created something or how you can take control of a situation and be at cause.

Cause – Why?	Effect – What?

Accountability and *responsibility* come from the understanding of *Cause* and *Effect*.

There are also a few more exercises that I would like to share with you on how to accept responsibility for your actions or behaviours. To be truly accountable for our results, we have to dig deep. We have to understand how we go to where we are. We have to understand why we have made assumptions and labelled certain people or situations, triggering an impact on our results.

Let's take our power back by taking ownership of our mistakes. Did you know that when you doubt or when you are not at cause, you give your power to doubt and therefore your power to resolution and change?

When you doubt your power, you give your power to your doubt. –
Honore de Balzac

Believe in yourself and believe in your ability to empower every situation. With just the right mindset, you can create massive changes in your life.

THE MIRROR EXERCISE

A way to loosen up the boundaries between you and another person is trying the mirror exercise.

1) Problem	2) Opposite of problem
4) Reflect mirror on other	3) Look into the mirror

Write down your problem in box 1. Example: My partner doesn't show me love.

Now, in box 2, write the opposite. My partner is always showing me love.

Next, hold up a mirror. Take ownership and be accountable for the problem.

In box 3, you might write: I am not showing love.

In box 4, reflect on the person you are having the problem with. Following our example, say they are not showing love.

What are your insights?

The mirror exercise tells us that we create all our circumstances in our environment and loved ones. It's a very powerful tool to use and a great way to be at cause or to be accountable for the way you think and feel.

HOW WE CONSTRUCT REALITY?

- We create what we observe
- We observe with our minds
- Observations are measurements
- Measurements transform nothing into something...this is how we get ourselves into unnecessary pickles.

We make measurements through our own language and labels of how we see the situation to be. However, if we dissect a problem, it helps us diffuse it. Dissecting allows us to see that quite often the problem or story that we have in our mind either doesn't really exist or that it is has been fabricated.

Continuing the example from our previous exercise, let's dive into the reality of it all.

The statement or problem we are working with – *My partner does not love me.*

A = my partner

B = does not love me

If we use this statement through the below quadrants, what do you get?

                                                    + Positive

-AB (negative positive)	AB (positive positive)
What wouldn't happen if you did?	What would happen if you did?
Example – What wouldn't happen if your partner did love you?	*Example – What would happen if your partner did love you?*
-A-B (negative negative)	**A-B (positive negative)**
What wouldn't happen if you didn't?	What would happen if you didn't?
Example – What wouldn't happen if your partner didn't love you?	*Example – What would happen if you didn't love your partner?*

                                                    - Negative

By stepping back and evaluating the situation, this gives us an opportunity to unscramble a way of thinking and reprogram the labels we have on people or situations.

This is another great tool to solve any conflicting outcomes. By going through this exercise, you may find you are not congruent with your current situations. Therefore, this may bring up other possible new problems to light. You may find you are sabotaging an outcome or simply that your needs are unfulfilled.

Ask yourself, if you *make this change*

- What will happen?
- What won't happen?

And...if you *don't make this change*

- What will happen?
- What won't happen?

MASLOW'S HIERARCHY OF NEEDS

In 1943, psychologist Abraham H. Maslow stated that people are motivated to achieve certain needs. When one need is fulfilled, a person seeks to fulfil the next one and so on.

The earliest and most widespread version of Maslow's (1943 - 1954) hierarchy of needs includes:

Biological and Physiological needs

- Air
- Food
- Drink
- Shelter
- Warmth
- Sex
- Sleep

Safety needs

- Protection from elements
- Freedom from fear
- Security
- Order
- Law
- Stability

Love and belongingness needs

- Friendship
- Intimacy
- Affection
- Love (from work group, family, friends, romantic relationships)

Esteem needs

- Self-esteem
- Achievement
- Self-respect
- Respect from others
- Mastery
- Independence
- Status
- Dominance
- Prestige
- Managerial responsibility

Cognitive needs

- Knowledge
- Meaning

Aesthetic needs

- Appreciation
- Search for beauty
- Balance
- Form

Self-actualisation needs

- Realising personal potential
- Self-fulfilment
- Seeking personal growth
- Peak experiences

Transcendence needs

- Helping others to achieve self-actualisation

RECALLING MEMORIES

Our minds are notoriously prone to errors, hasty assumptions and false memories. Our perceptual system is not built to notice absolutely everything within our environment. We absorb information through our 5 senses; there will be bits or gaps that we will miss.

As a result, when remembering an event or a situation, your *recall* of memories or experiences may be false memories. They might have been created by your brain because of its inability to deal with all the information at any given moment.

The fact is that, after an event has occurred, we create a memory from that event. Obviously, that memory is made out of pictures, sounds, people, emotions and the state that you were in at that very time.

The next time that you recall that memory, you will be recalling the memory itself – because it's the first recall. If you attempt to recall the memory again a couple of years down the track, this second recall will not be of the initial memory. According to research, it will be a recall of the first recall.

In other words, our memories are a false construction. They have been distorted by the number of times we recall that memory. Our memories look, feel and change depending on the current state we are in when we recall our initial memory or what we *think* to be the first memory. In fact, it may be the second or third recall, depending on how many times you have recalled that particular memory.

'Recalling your memories actually alters the memory itself.'

WHY WORRY?

Be proactive, not reactive. After exercising accountability, it is also important to understand what we have control over and what is a waste of our time and energy.

Our worries are of our own making. We create them in our own minds, through our inability or failure to understand and fully appreciate our feelings.

One of my mentors said, *'worrying is like praying for what you don't want'*. That will always resonate in my mind. My default position then was to worry all the time; worry about my son, my partner, my animals, my family and the list goes on, but never about me.

Most of the times the things we worry about, never actually happen. Think about it; have you ever made yourself sick from worrying about a job interview, getting approved for house loan or your partner agreeing to have a child?

Let's put pen to paper and create a list of what you worry about. Write down everything that keeps you up at night.

Next to your list of worries, write down the percentage of control you have over each one. For example, a part of your list may look like this.

- Dogs' health – 0%
- Son's wellbeing – 0%
- Partner getting a job – 0%
- Family having enough money – 0%
- Parents' health – 0%
- Big bills – 10%

As you can see from my above list, a lot of the things I worry about I have no control over. But what if we apply the rule of accountability and responsibility and only focus on what we have control over? What would your list look like then?

PLANNING MAKES PERFECT

To plan in life is to be accountable. As I quite often mention in this book, how we all live such a fast pace life, the time that we take out to *plan* our day is what makes it productive. If you wake up first thing in the morning and check your mobile device, jump into the shower, get ready for work and respond to emails as soon as you sit at your desk, what kind of day do you think you are going to have? A very reactive one! And...at the mercy of your surroundings.

Now picture this. You get up in the morning, get ready for work and then arrive to sit at your desk, without having a peak at your mobile device and without turning on your computer. You sit there for 5 minutes and plan your day. How will your day be? Proactive!

Personally, I make a list of 3 things that I have to complete by the day. They are my total focus. Then, I will have another 3 things as a second priority, in case I do have some spare time on my hands. Being proactive and planning my day is so much more empowering. I have a much more productive day, without being at the mercy of others. I plan, delegate what I need to delegate and at the end, I am accountable and responsible for my day.

CHAPTER 13
CHALLENGE YOUR ASSUMPTIONS

"Expectation feeds frustration. It is an unhealthy attachment to people, things and outcomes we wish we could control, but don't." –
Dr. Steve Maraboli

FROM EXPECTATIONS TO FRUSTRATIONS

You know the feeling; that build-up of annoyance, wanting to change the circumstances you find yourself in, but knowing that you can't? Wanting something more than you ended up with? Predicting an outcome that didn't go your way?

That feeling is frustration fed by expectations.

We all have expectations. It's part of human nature. Unfortunately, they inevitably lead to discontent. To be perfectly honest, we're better off without them, because – and here's the real crux of the matter – more often than not, expectations lead to disappointment. If we can choose to live a life without disappointment, why wouldn't we?

When you drop all expectations, you will:

- Be happier
- Never be disappointed
- Approach all situations with an open mind

When you find yourself getting wound up, you need to stop. Pause. Ask yourself a couple of essential questions:

- What are my expectations of this situation?
- Are my expectations realistic?
- Why do I have expectations of an outcome?
- Am I in control of the outcome?

When we identify our expectations in this way, we give ourselves the opportunity to challenge or change our thinking. The quickest, easiest way to do this is to trade our expectations for appreciation. Trust me, when you do this successfully, the world changes instantly, for quite a few reasons. Primarily, because you're shifting your mindset from *wanting* to *accepting* to *being grateful*. That's a great start. But it's also an important moment for growth, as it provides a perfect opportunity to consider *why* you feel a certain way and learn more about yourself.

Assumptions – our blind spots

'When I met you, I said hello to the possibility of forever.'

Don't believe everything you think!

To put it shortly, an assumption is something that is accepted as true or certain to happen without proof.

Assumptions are the termites of any relationship. Don't be afraid to challenge your assumptions; things are not always what they seem.

Most of the time, an assumption is us supposing or presuming a certain outcome or belief. In reality, we are just guessing or hypnotising what we deem to be true without evidence. It is only just a thought or an interpretation or what we have speculated or surmised.

The action of taking on power or responsibility is *not* to assume. It's about accepting that there are different ways of seeing and understanding every situation.

Reverse your assumptions

A creative way to turn things around is to probe your brain to think differently about your assumptions. It's quite easy; we just need to reverse them to give them a different perspective. Let's give it a go.

- What is your assumption about a problem?
- What is the challenge about this assumption?

Write your assumptions down in the first column and then reverse your assumptions into the column beside.

Assumption	Reverse Assumption	New idea about Assumption
You have to work hard to earn money.	You don't have to work hard to earn money.	Working smarter by investing time that is well spent for money – What can I do as a business that will bring passive income?
Relationships are hard work.	Relationships are easy.	Remain an individual in a relationship allowing space for freedom – What can I do to create balance in my relationship so to make it easy?
If I buy a house, I won't be able to travel overseas.	If I buy a house, I will be able to travel overseas.	I purchase a property to get into the market and lease it out for a year while I travel. I then have tenants paying for the mortgage while I am travelling.
If I start my own business, I won't earn enough to support the family.	If I start my own business, I will have enough money to support my family.	I will have part-time work or full-time work while I am building my company, until I generate enough income for me to make the transition.

Assumptions can be quite limiting, holding you back. However, if you deep dive and unpack your assumptions, you will probe your brain to come up with something more creative. It will create movement and ideas by challenging your assumptions. You give it a go now.

Assumption	Reverse Assumption	New idea about Assumption

Here are some universal truths:

- Everyone has his or her own particular view of the world
- 2 people can look at the exact same thing and see something totally different
- Understanding that we each have different perspectives of the world is the essence of letting go of expectations

It was the character Atticus Finch in *Harper Lee's* best-selling novel *'To Kill a Mockingbird'* who said it like this: *"You never really understand a person until you consider things from his point of view – until you climb into his skin and walk around in it."*

Basically, if we want to *connect* and *communicate* with each other, then we need to stand in each other's shoes – at least for a moment or two, once in a while.

Having an understanding of another person's view of the world doesn't necessarily require agreement. It simply requires acknowledgement. It helps you to respect their choices. In the end, it sets you up for more successful communication.

PEOPLE ARE NOT THEIR BEHAVIOURS

Next time you feel tempted to make a comment or label someone based on his or her behaviour, remember that this is not an ideal way to *connect* and develop a healthy relationship.

Try challenging the *behaviour* instead of the person.

When someone does something that really confronts your feelings or perspective, instead of reacting or lashing out, ask them if everything is alright.

This is a powerful conversation starter. It enables you to open a dialogue. It provides you with an avenue for saying how you feel about the behaviour. It also leads to open discussion that can have a massive impact on relationships.

As human beings, our behaviours are unpredictable. They change all the time and are often influenced by other factors. At times when we are reactive, defensive or volatile, these behaviours can be an important indicator that we're stressed or tired, or have other things going on that we need to address to find calm and balance again. When others are behaving this way, if we can look past the behaviours and see the person, we're in a better position to effectively communicate and relate.

It's important to remember that most behaviours are unconscious. We don't always stop, pause and consider what we're doing. Whenever you experience an emotion, feel anxious or overwhelmed for no apparent reason, you know something is going on deep in your unconscious mind.

Even the language or words you use are a hint or clue to what is going on unconsciously, if only you stop to listen to yourself.

> *"I have not failed. I have found just 10,000 ways that won't work."* –
> **Thomas Edison**

We are all doing the best we can with the resources we have (this includes you).

It's easy to be judgmental and critical of other people, friends and families. What about a little bit of appreciation, compassion, understanding and most of all, acceptance? This is harder to practice, but when we do, the rewards are wonderful.

When we stop taking things personally and move to a mindset of accepting others as they are – based on the assumption that we are all doing the best we can with what we know and what we have – then automatically we change the way we are feeling and thinking. By doing this, we can change the way we experience the world. It opens up new opportunities and possibilities for better relationships and richer experiences, and makes life a whole lot more enjoyable.

THERE IS NO FAILURE, ONLY FEEDBACK

When our expectations are not met, we end up feeling failure.

But what if there was no failure, and only feedback?

Labelling or judging anything as a *'failure'* sets you up for – guess what – more failure. It's a fact that your focus on failure will bring you more of it. However, if you focus on what you can do differently, you'll be able to yield better results in what you are trying to achieve. Remove the sense of emotion and be objective.

The value here is seeing all information as feedback. Feedback opens up *creativity* and *possibility*. It creates an open mind, and an open mind is one that is able to receive new information, work out how to do things differently and strive for a better outcome.

Failure is almost looked upon as a dead end, in a sort of *'there's nothing more I can do here'* kind of way. It's completely negative. And it is energy defeating.

> *"Failure is simply the opportunity to begin again, this time more intelligently."* – **Henry Ford**

Feedback, on the other hand, opens up opportunities that create renewed energy and vigour.

Feedback empowers us to re-do a task until we succeed. Feedback allows us to gather more intelligence, seek advice and gain more experience. Feedback enables us to learn from our mistakes. Feedback is positive.

Eventually, we will habitually believe that there is no such thing as failure and, in due course, we will refrain from failing altogether!

THE MOST FLEXIBLE PERSON WINS

The easy trick to a life that's fulfilling and rewarding beyond measure is flexibility.

It's that simple.

Flexibility is a kind of in-built resilience, helping you know when to change direction, employ new tactics or have the courage to start again. Ironically, the more flexible you are, the more accepting you are of change and the more open you are to possibility, then the more control you have over your life.

Being adaptable and being able to make the most of what you have allows you to tap into different circumstances, opportunities and choices. When you are stubborn, you limit your results.

While we can't control external situations and events, we are capable of controlling our own reactions and responses to them.

If we keep doing the same old, same old, and not applying the act of *flexibility*, then we keep on being reactive and getting the same results. An individual who is flexible will always change their behaviour whenever something goes wrong. This kind of versatility opens up productivity, possibility and an ongoing sense of wonder and curiosity about what might happen next.

Our greatest power and potential as human beings is our ability to learn and grow. So, give it a go. Open yourself up to new and interesting prospects instead of being stuck and rigid in your ways. You're already reading this book, and changing one's own behaviour is really just about finding new solutions to difficult situations.

EVERYTHING IS POSSIBLE

If it were possible in the world and therefore possible for me, then what kind of life would I lead?

Isn't this a great question?

If you could *be* anything, *do* anything, *have* anything.

Well, you can. It's just a matter of making it happen.

Possibility can transform your life and everything in it. This is not just the stuff of daydreams; possibility can open your mind to new opportunities, a new way of thinking and working out how you can go about to achieving what it is that you want to achieve. Anything and everything is *possible,* with discipline.

When you surround yourself with people who share the same mindset and assumption that all is possible, then you increase your desire and belief that all is possible.

RESPONSES ARE BASED ON EXPERIENCE

Our assumptions, beliefs and expectations are all internal representations. What this means is that they are not necessarily an accurate reflection of what is occurring in the external world. While we believe we are looking at the external situation and seeing it clearly, how we represent things in our mind...is our own interpretation, not the reality. These interpretations determine how we react as well as how we experience every moment. Therefore, they lay the foundation of our experiences as our reality.

What follows then is that we actually have a choice regarding how we interpret our experiences and, subsequently, how we interpret *reality* in its present form.

Our interpretations come from our experiences and everything that has happened to us in our lifetime.

So what might happen then if we gave our interpretations a new meaning?

In any given situation, if we develop the discipline to *pause* and ask ourselves what *else* can something mean, we can provide ourselves with a content or context reframe (Chapter 1).

We each have a unique map of our own *reality*, and it is different to everyone around us. Furthermore, we have a choice; we can choose to change our reality map to provide us greater results. The way to do this is to explore other possible scenarios and explanations at any given time. By using imagination and creativity, we can alter our in-built, unconscious, autopilot responses.

Over time, because the brain is such an amazing organ, we can start to actually build up a new library of responses.

PEOPLE WORK PERFECTLY

No one is broken and no one needs fixing. While we can all do with a little *'tune up'* once in a while, each and every one of us has the resources they need to make the changes they want to.

We all function in a perfect manner, even if we are not getting the results we want from our lives. When we dig deep within ourselves and make a conscious effort to actually understand our make-up, then we start to tap into our greatest power as human beings: our potential to change, adapt, renew and learn.

We can't *'fix'* other people, either. In fact, people carry out their own behavioural strategies excellently. It's just that sometimes those strategies are flawed: poorly designed, ineffective and even counter-productive. What you need to worry about are your strategies and whether or not they are working for you or are they appropriate ones for the new life you're creating for yourself.

RESPECT IS PARAMOUNT

To show respect, even to those who are not worthy of it, is a reflection of your character. It's true that not everybody deserves respect; understanding that is simply an act of honouring your own personal boundaries. If you compromise these, you compromise your own self-respect.

If someone does something that you think violates your code of ethics or conduct, and you can't work it out through open, honest discussion, then perhaps it's time to rethink the relationship and its purpose in your life. Sometimes we need to let people and relationships go, in order to thrive. This too opens more room for us to attract what we want.

Nevertheless, it's a challenge. It requires constant mindfulness because when we switch to *'autopilot'*, our actions become unconscious. These are often the actions that do not serve us well.

When we slip from mindfulness, we slip into the *'same old'* and then we find ourselves judging others and forming expectations.

> Respect is earned. Honesty is appreciated. Trust is gained. Loyalty is returned. Respect is for those who deserve it, not for those who demand it. But remember, that includes you: Respect your SELF!

Our actions are not random. We are always trying to achieve something better and something greater, even though we may not be aware of it. It's a basic human instinct to *'move forward for the betterment of self'*, ingrained in us from the moment we are born; we learn to eat, walk and talk. Every behaviour – yours and other people's – has a positive intention behind it, so continue to assume this; sidestep negativity and watch your life transform.

The learning is in the doing.

CHAPTER 14
REPROGRAM YOUR UNCONSCIOUS DRIVERS

'You can reinvent yourself as often as you want. The only thing that is stopping you is you!'

Would you believe me if I told you that most of the time *we have no idea* why we do what we do?

It's true.

If you take a long look over your own life and take the time to be really honest with yourself, you'll see that you have particular *patterns* that often show up in your behaviour and your decision-making. Like our unconscious thoughts and our unconscious behaviour, these are formed very early in our lives, as discussed in Chapter 3.

These similarities in what we do and how we do it repeat again and again and again. The situations we find ourselves in might be different, but the way we behave and the way we think remain the same.

Why do we do this? Because of our *unconscious drivers.*

Sometimes, they can be useful. But a lot of the time, when we take a good look at *why* we do what we do, then we realise that they are not serving our best interests. Sometimes they're hindering us, even holding us back.

Unconscious drivers work a little bit like this:

> *'When you don't know what you don't know and don't even know that you don't know it, you're in a state of 'unconscious incompetence'.*

A big mouthful of words, but they make a very important point. Whenever you're starting something new, whether it is sitting for a driver's license, sewing with a machine for the very first time or even starting a new job, you begin by being incompetent.

Basically, you're ignorant, inexpert and unskilled at this particular new thing.

A toddler sitting in the back seat while his parent is driving the car does not know what he doesn't know and doesn't even know it. You see?

From that state we progress to *'conscious incompetence'* – the point where we realise that this new job or activity is something that we actually don't know how to do – we become aware that there are possibly rules and skills that we need to understand, learn and apply.

When we start learning new skills, we move to a stage of *'conscious competence'*. Essentially, at this point we're learning, but have not yet mastered the skills we need. When learning to drive, this is the phase where you can actually drive, but you're conscious at every step of the process. So much so, that if you had a passenger you might ask them not to talk to you because you need to be able to have total focus and concentration. This is *'conscious competence'*.

Finally, we reach *'unconscious competence'*. Now the skills have become embedded into our mind. We have created a habit and the information required has moved from the conscious mind in the front part of the brain, to the back of the mind. At this point, you're really confident and comfortable. So much so that one day you're driving from point A to point B, and when you get there you actually don't remember it! It is thanks to your *'unconscious driver'* that you got to the destination.

In many ways, we're lucky that we have unconscious drivers. Just imagine how much energy we would need to use, if we were to be conscious of absolutely everything we do. We'd be exhausted!

But *'unconscious drivers'* always occur in a sequence of internal and external representations that produce a specific outcome. Basically, they give us strategies for everything we learn to do, from maths, to sports, to decision-making, relaxation, attention, wealth, spelling, communication, love, eating, happiness, having fun and the list goes on. Whatever you can think of, we learn a strategy to do this. Once we have learned the strategy, then it goes into the filing system in the unconscious part of the mind.

The *power for change* comes when we access these unconscious drivers and then redesign them. You might not want to unlearn how to drive, but you might want to re-learn new ways of conducting relationships, relaxing, working and creating wealth. And because we can reengineer these unconscious drivers, we can give them a different meaning and impetus.

THE STRATEGIC MIND

'It's about planning your destiny.'

When we talk about how the mind works and *'strategies'*, we refer to the way our brain associates one thing with another and provides us with an internal representation of our external experience of reality. These strategies regulate how our brain pays attention to things.

For example, let's have a look at a *buying strategy* – at how the brain functions when we shop. If you find yourself having a giggle as you're reading this, then that's a sure sign that you are connected with your drivers. This is really good because, as a general rule, we are not conscious of our strategies or our drivers until we slow down, pause and actually observe how we behave or, play out our strategy.

Motivation

Our first *buying strategy* is *motivation*. This is the *'hook'*. Shoes are a good example to use because they are not always a practical purchase. Often, they are completely unnecessary (you can, after all, only wear one pair at a time!), but often the driver is visual – see it, want it, buy it. This kind of shopping can get expensive.

Some people apply certain criteria to the shoes they buy. For instance, the shoes need to be *pink*. They need to have a *high heel*. They need to be *vintage* looking. This kind of motivation is driven by an *inner voice* or *internal dialogue* and these kinds of shoppers look at the *facts* and *figures of a purchase*. Even a price may be associated at times, like a budget for the purchase.

Other shoppers buy, based on how they *feel*. The shoes they choose need to be comfortable and provide some tactile pleasure.

There are other motivators too. Some people will purchase shoes by the way they *sound*, or the way they *smell*. These drivers are less common, but they do exist. I have never heard of anyone who buys shoes for taste, but it's possible. What you'll notice is that these motivations are very much driven by our senses:

- Visual – you see the shoes, you buy them
- Auditory – you like the sound of the shoes
- Kinaesthetic – you like the feeling of the shoes
- Auditory digital – you have criteria for the shoes
- Olfactory – you like the smell of the shoes
- Gustatory – you like the taste of the shoes. In a world full of 7 billion people, this is entirely possible.

After motivation comes the decision to buy.

Decision

Decision-making is not the same for everybody. Your decision might be *automatic* – you just go ahead and buy the shoes without too much thought. People who favour automatic decision-making can sometimes find themselves with wardrobes full of things they have never worn, simply because their decision was instant and not backed up by too much thought.

People who are not automatic decision-makers might have a different sort of purchasing *'rule'*. For example, you might need to be convinced on 3 separate occasions that the shoes are a good buy. This would mean 3 trips to the shop to look at the shoes try on the shoes and finally buy the shoes. A lot of time and effort for a pair of shoes!

Imagine if you were conscious of this behaviour. If you actually understood these aspects about yourself and were able to apply some self-control over making snap decisions. Or...instead of having to convince yourself 3 times on 3 different occasions, you just went and mulled them over while having a coffee?

Some people love the *'but wait...there's more!'* meaning, they love a bargain or a bundle buy. Just can't resist. Other people need to sleep on purchasing decisions, not just overnight, but for a few nights, giving themselves time to really think things over. Then there are those shoppers who just never make decisions. Ever! These people are never quite convinced that it's going to be the right purchase. They can do all the research, find the cheapest price, know all about competitive products on offer, and still not buy. Every time they set out to purchase, they follow the same pattern or decision-driver: information gathering, comparison, shopping around for the best price and finally, walk away. These shoppers are excellent at saving money!

Then there's the reassurance phase, after the purchase itself – the admiration and the compliments for your new shoes. The approval from others that you got a *'bargain'* or that your excellent taste led you to make an enviable purchase. This is a driver too.

Understanding

We all have different, unconscious drivers that have us acting on a sort of *'auto pilot'*. If you understand this, it's a little easier to find the patience for dealing with other people who can be very different from yourself. Actually sometimes, when you know what you're looking for, watching how other people behave can be fun!

The drivers that direct our decisions, behaviours, actions and interactions with the world around us essentially determine *how* our brain pays attention, as well as *what* it pays attention to. It's a form of pattern recognition – the brain attempts to sort through what the body is sensing and experiencing.

Imagine your brain is your computer and your drivers are the software programs that run the applications in your mind. The software directs your thoughts, beliefs, values, memories and responses. These unconscious mental programs run our lives at an unconscious level of awareness. These mental programs determine how we decide what information we delete, distort and/or generalise from our experience.

Basically, these programs determine how we process information.

So when it is explained like this, you can start to grasp just how much *influence* these programs have over the way we behave from one minute to the next. Everything we do. Everything! The brain processes information based on these unconscious drivers that are running in the background of our minds. This is how we make sense of the world around us and how we form our own beliefs, opinions and perspectives about the world, our life and our circumstances.

The upshot is that when you better understand your own unconscious drivers, you can better understand yourself and your own psychological tendencies.

How you make sense of the world and how you make decisions, how you interpret your life and circumstances and how you interact with others will all begin to make sense once you understand what drivers are influencing your brain. Once you've figured this out, you will have a great deal of insight into your values, beliefs, convictions, habits, behaviours and, yes, those self-sabotaging patterns too.

When it comes to unconscious drivers, they can be very strong, not easy to reshape or let go of. It can be useful to ask yourself the following questions:

- How useful and effective are they?

- How are they shaping my life and circumstances?

- Given my desired outcomes, are they helpful or hurtful?

- Do I need to make any changes? Why? Why not?

UNCONSCIOUS DRIVERS AND MOTIVATIONS

Out of sight – out of mind...

There are no inappropriate behaviours, only inappropriate contexts.

Reading people in an effort to understand their drivers can be lots of fun, but more than that, it puts you in a place of compassion, understanding and patience. And more often than not, it teaches you a thing or 2 about the way you behave as well!

This section is designed to help you understand more about unconscious drivers and perhaps bring forward your own conscious awareness of what they are. The first driver is our *direction driver*.

Direction driver

There are 2 direction drivers: *moving towards* and *moving away*. Another way to look at this is to think about *pain* and *pleasure* – when we put them together, we are motivated by moving away from pain or moving towards pleasure.

Let's do a quick example around losing weight (a lot of people can relate to this one). Have you ever gone on a diet or eating regimen? If you have, was it because you did not want to be fat (i.e. moving away from the pain of being fat)? Or was it because you wanted to be healthy and vibrant (i.e. moving towards the pleasure of feeling good)?

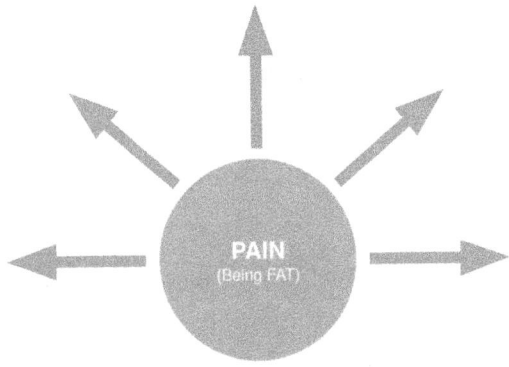

Figure 1: Moving Away Motivation

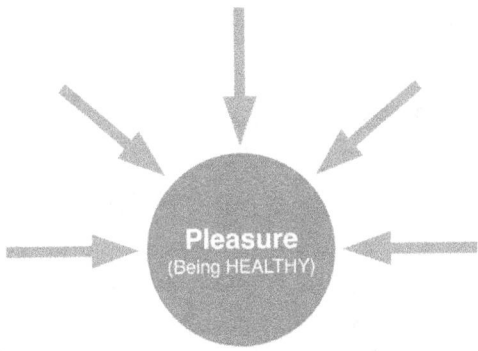

Figure 2: Moving Towards Motivation

By looking at the 2 illustrations above, who do you think can hold the focus and motivation for longer? I am sure you will agree with me that the person with only one possible direction will remain focused on achieving their goal.

Someone *moving towards* this ideal of losing weight is:

- Energised by accomplishment
- Positive and motivated
- Confident about achieving their goal

- Driven by the reward in the end
- Focused on the possibility and benefit

Someone *moving away* from this ideal of losing weight is:

- Negative and feels pain
- Talking about the terrible things that no longer serve them
- Motivated by threats like potential problems
- Frightened of taking risks
- Sometimes overcautious and miss the opportunity

Looking at the example of taking on the challenge of losing weight, the person with the *moving away* driver would focus on (or say) the following comments:

- I don't want to be fat.
- I don't want to look bad.
- I am afraid that my partner will leave me, if I don't lose the weight.
- I hate going to the gym. It physically hurts.
- I don't want to be sick anymore.

The person with a *moving towards* driver would speak like this:

- I am creating a plan to lose 2 kg per week.
- I am working towards my overall health.
- I have joined a gym close to where I live/work.
- I am setting myself a challenge to lose 15 kg by September 27th (very specific).
- I am so excited and so motivated that I can't sleep.

Can you see the difference between the 2? One is moving away from what they want to achieve and one is moving towards what they want to achieve.

The key is to understand the driver that motivates the thought patterns and behaviour. Then, we can communicate with that person in a way that kick-starts their ignition, which appeals to their driving force and creates motion.

Moving Away or Moving Towards: Understand and Apply

It is actually very simple; let's stay with the losing weight example. Imagine you are a personal trainer and you have a *moving away* client. You can simply say – *"if you don't do something about your weight now, your life could be shortened by 10 years"* (using fear to get them motivated). Or if your client was a self-motivated, *moving forward* person, you can say – *"are you ready to kick your health to the next level?"*

When talking to someone with a *move away* driver, you could say something like *"here is what we want to avoid"* or *"this will reduce our potential problem"*.

People who have this driver notice what should be avoided, gotten rid of or fixed. They have a tendency to focus on problems and the things that they must avoid before moving forward. These individuals are good at troubleshooting, solving problems and pinpointing possible obstacles. They may set goals; however, they have difficulty prioritising their actions and are often distracted by trying to fix crisis situations. In order to influence, motivate and build connection with a move away person, you need to present them with a problem that needs to get fixed and then hold them accountable for solving this problem. This really appeals to them.

They tend to fall into yo-yo style results simply because once they have moved so far away from their pain point (i.e. being fat), the motivation disappears and they slowly start making their way back into the pain zone.

For a *move towards* person, you would say something along the lines of *"here are our goals and objectives"*. People with this driver firmly focus on the attainment of their goals. They tend to be good at managing priorities and are always clear about what they want out of life. In order to influence, motivate and build a sincere connection with a *move towards* person, it's important to focus their mind on the process of goal achievement – inform them about the significance of achieving specific goals, outcomes and the benefits, particularly the benefits to themselves.

Action driver

When you come into a situation, do you usually act quickly after sizing it up? Or do you step back a little and conduct your own assessment of the consequences before you act?

If you're not sure, then think of a recent situation where you've had to deal with a problem or make a decision and look carefully at how you assessed the situation and acted upon it. You'll find that you're either *proactive* or *reactive*.

Proactive people

- Initiate change and shape the future
- Take charge and get things done
- Take action to prevent problems or fires from starting
- Plan and prepare
- Are drawn to sales or working for themselves

Reactive people

- Respond to situations or changes in the environment
- Are people who fight the fire after it has started
- Act on emergencies
- Wait for others to take lead or take action only when the time is right
- May wait until the last minute to take action

A *proactive driver* will always be in a state of mind of controlling all of the possible things they can control. If something comes up that they can't do anything about, they're unlikely to waste time and energy on it. They're into planning and creating action, and they like to see results.

On the other hand, someone with a *reactive driver* will worry about the things they can't control, and tend to act only once things have hit the fan.

Relationship driver

Think for a moment and ask yourself, what is the relationship between the career/job you are doing this year and what you did this time last year? Have you moved forward? Have you stayed still? Are you working on the same projects? Are you focused on something different? Have you changed jobs completely?

There are 2 drivers here, *sameness* and *difference*.

Sameness

A person with a *sameness driver* is often optimistic, very approving and tends to look for similarities and common ground when communicating with other people. These people often base their decisions on the similarities they see in others, in circumstances and in life. If you are looking for a way to influence, motivate and connect with this person, you will need to listen intently and find common ground. Mirroring their experiences, beliefs, values and perceptions will help you to develop a strong emotional bond and greater levels of connection.

People who like sameness:

- Are motivated by stability and security
- Ask how things are similar or share common features
- Are uncomfortable with change
- 'Delete' a lot of things that they can't relate to

Difference

A person with a *difference driver* often tends to go against the grain. They tend to find faults in things, in circumstances and in others. They always look for differences and will tend to disagree with you no matter what you do or say. Therefore, in order to influence, motivate and connect with this person, you will need to become proficient at using reverse psychology.

People attracted by difference:

- Love different places, people and experiences
- Ask how things are distinct or unique
- Embrace change
- Loves variety and uncertainty

How does this help you? Well, let's see through an example. Imagine a couple; one has a *sameness* driver and the other a *difference* driver. Let's say, they are trying to decide on a restaurant for the night – the *sameness* driver would want to go to the Thai place down the road that they *always* go to and the *difference* driver would like to try something completely different. What could a possible solution be? Taking turns!

This is handy information to improve your relationship, because you then would appreciate each other's differences and accommodate accordingly.

Focus driver

If we were going to do a project together, would you want to know the big picture first or the details?

Figuring this out is really fun, and it's a handy tool in the workplace because it helps you to work more effectively with your colleagues once you know what *'drives'* them. Do you remember when we talked about *'Chunking-Up'* (big picture) and *'"Chunking-Down"'* (detailed)? Well, here you will learn how to use this to your advantage when looking at motivating other people.

Global

- Generalists who prefer the big picture and broad strokes
- They don't want to miss seeing the woods for the trees
- Tend to forget about the little details
- Can be impatient
- Can switch off, if there's too much specific information being given to them

Detail

- Have a strong preference for small, specific bits of information
- Pay *big* attention to *small* details, because they believe that even a tiny hole can sink a big ship
- Become frustrated with overviews and summaries, if there's not enough attention paid to the finer points

Now, you understand that if you are a detailed person and you are having a conversation with a global person, you could quite quickly put them to sleep or they lose complete concentration. Whereas, if you knew they were global, you could give them the big picture first and allow space or time for them to ask you questions if they want more information. This applies the other way around too.

Frame of reference driver

This driver relates to how we measure ourselves against others in the world around us. It's our frame of reference for how we go to work, in relationships, in our lives, in general. In this context, there are 2 drivers, one *internal* and one *external*.

Internal

A person with an *internal frame* of reference is very intuitive and self-oriented. This means that they often make decisions based on personal feelings and opinions. They must feel within themselves that they've done a good job or made a good decision. If you're looking for a successful way to influence, motivate and connect with this person, you will need to talk about their experiences and allow them to make up their own mind about the issue at hand.

People with an *internally* focused driver:

- Have their own criteria for making judgments within themselves
- Able to stay motivated even when the chips are down
- May often ignore good advice from others

External

A person with an *external frame* of reference is very much focused on others. They are consistently seeking external answers and approval from others. As a result, they make decisions based on people's opinions, perspectives and actions. Motivating and connecting authentically with this person means that you need to provide them with your own suggestions, or talk to them about other people's ideas and ask them how they can be of value in this situation.

People who have an *externally* focused driver:

- Rely on feedback to make decisions and to function effectively
- Are good team players
- Can be indecisive and unmotivated when there is little feedback

Reason driver

This relates to *why* you're choosing to do what you are doing. The reason driver breaks into 2 categories: the *possibility* driver and the *necessity* driver.

The *necessity* and *possibility* drivers are based on whether a person makes decisions based on *necessity* or primarily based on *possibility*.

Possibility

The person who has the p*ossibility* driver puts emphasis on the realm of opportunities and options; they would say something like *'we really can do this!'*.

They truly believe that anything could happen and that anything is possible – they are infectious about their enthusiasm.

- They believe the world is their oyster
- They have control over their lives and choices
- They are optimistic, action-orientated and enthusiastic

They often use language like – *'I can achieve this, it's just a matter of planning'* or *'anything is possible if you believe it'*. Quite often they say yes to everything, even if they don't know how, and work out how to do it later. They use words like, *'I will'*, *'I can'*, *'I create'*, *'I believe'* and that *'I can achieve anything I put my mind to'*.

A person with a *possibility* based driver often seeks variety and opportunity. These people primarily make decisions that are based on gaining pleasure. They don't particularly like to settle for less than what they really, really want in life. They are motivated to look for possibilities that will help them expand their opportunities.

If you want to influence, motivate and connect with this person, you need to present them with challenges, ideals, inspirations as well as informing them about the risks they need to take to get to the end result, but the inevitable opportunities that will be available once they have reached that point.

Necessity

Necessity people do what they have to do, their thought processes operate along the lines of: *'well, I have to pay the bills'*, *'but I need a job close to home, so this will do'* etc.

- They can be in danger of limiting their choices to the restricted options presented to them, rather than going out to look for opportunities and options
- They will do what needs to be done because obligation and duties drive them
- They often settle for what life gives them

They primarily make decisions that are based on avoiding *'pain'* or *'change'*. They will settle for what's available and don't care much about options or varied experiences.

If you're looking for a way to influence, motivate and connect with this person, you will need to focus on making them feel secure and comfortable with their decisions. Provide them with something that's familiar, easy and safe.

Option driver

A person with an *option driver* is motivated by the possibility to do something in another way. They are the type of people who will develop procedures and then not follow them. They enjoy breaking or bending the rules, exploring new ideas and possibilities. They may start a new project and not feel compelled to finish it. To motivate and influence these people, you need to use words like – opportunity, alternatives, break the rules, flexibility, variety, and unlimited possibilities, and expand your choices and options. These people do well in situations that require them to find solutions or alternatives to current systems.

Options

- Enjoy trying out new ways of doing things
- Love variety and options
- Good at starting projects; may not see them through
- Don't ask options to drive unless you want to see the sights, like to take different routes each time

A person with more of a *procedure driver* likes to follow a set rules or processes. Once they understand a procedure, they will repeat it over and over again. They have great difficulty developing new processes and without a clearly defined procedure, they feel lost or stuck. They are more concerned about *how* to do something than *why* they should do it. Bending or breaking rules is heresy! They are motivated by words, such as doing it the correct or right way and follow procedure to the letter.

Procedures

- Display a preference for following set methodologies
- Follow set rules and procedures
- Follow working procedures repeatedly without modification
- Stick to speed limits and take personal affront when other drivers use mobiles while driving with one hand

Affiliation driver

Your preferred style of working can reveal a lot about yourself too. Do you know what you need to do to be successful at work?

A person who has an *independent driver* is often introverted. They will rarely take immediate decisive action to get something done. Instead, they must think and reflect upon what they are about to do before taking action. Therefore, in order to influence, motivate and build connection with this person, you need to allow them time and space to reflect upon the decision they are about to make. Without this time and space, they will feel threatened and might resist taking action.

Independent workers

- Want sole responsibility for what they are doing
- Their work productivity and quality suffers with others around
- Prefer to work alone, in an office with the door closed
- Do not take directions well

A person who has a *team driver* is often very curious and focused on the needs of other people. So much so, that before they make any kind of decision, they will often think of what's in it for others and how others will benefit from this decision. In essence, they will put other people's needs ahead of their own. Therefore, in order to influence, motivate and build connection with this person, you will need to focus your conversation on the needs of others. Outline the benefits that other people will gain from this situation and how this could potentially improve their lives.

Team

- Want to share responsibility with others
- Dislikes working on their own
- Want their rewards to come from the team
- Want to do everything with their team
- If left to do something alone, these people will actually find others to be involved too

Attention direction driver

Where do you focus your attention when communicating with people?

You might not be aware of this, but when you're communicating, your attention can be focused outside of people or inside their thoughts.

A person with more of a *self-driver* can be self-centred and disassociated. These people make decisions based on their own personal interests – based on what's *'in it for them'* in any particular situation. As a result, in order to influence, motivate and build connection with this person, you will need to look at ways that can help you meet their needs. You must help them make a decision based on satisfying their own needs, wants and desires.

Self-directed people

- Attend to their own needs

- Are very in tune with their own thoughts, feelings, beliefs, preferences, ideas wants and needs
- Evaluate information based on how it affects them
- Make decisions about what is good for them long/short term

A person with more of a focus on *others driver* is often extroverted. They don't like to think about what they are going to do before doing it. Instead, they will just jump into things head first without much thought – working things out as they go along. In this situation, in order to influence, motivate and build connection with this person, you will need to get them to take decisive action. Encouraging constant involvement will keep them motivated and enthusiastic about the task at hand.

People driven by others

- Attend to others' values, beliefs, thoughts, feelings, needs and wants
- Nurture, value and develop others
- Consider the consequences of their actions and decisions by others in mind at all times
- Neglect their own needs and wants

CHANGING YOUR UNCONSCIOUS DRIVER

Sometimes, depending upon the situation or who else is involved in the interaction, you might find that you're a blend of 2 types of drivers. Having awareness of this is the first step towards change, and changing your unconscious driver can be easier than you might think.

We've talked often in this book about creating brain change in 21 days. This is no different – you're simply shifting how you process the world around you. While you might have spent your whole life looking at something from one perspective, changing that perspective is not impossible. With a plan, you can conquer and change your unconscious drivers too.

These unconscious drivers are simply habits. These habits were ingrained into our brain a long time ago, and they are supported by a set of beliefs and convictions. What you also need to understand is that these drivers are also likely to be underpinning your core values and beliefs. If that's the case, then you will certainly need to take into account all of the consequences that could result from making these changes.

So, it is imperative to *understand completely* **why** you might want to change these drivers. It might be as simple as these drivers are not supporting your goals. For example, you might want to take on a new role at work, but understand that big-picture thinking is required. You need to be less detail-focused and more *'globalist'* in your thinking.

Another example could be that you are in a relationship with a person who is a *sameness driver*, and you're a *different driver* who likes variety. Seeing things from 2 very different perspectives might be causing unnecessary stress and tension within your relationship. By understanding and acknowledging your conflicting drivers, you can mitigate a lot of problems.

These are just 2 of many reasons why changing your unconscious drivers can be helpful. But taking charge of the situation and initiating change within yourself requires you to have a good understanding of yourself, your situation and the other people involved so that you can determine the best path forward. This is something that only you can figure out. It takes a lot of *self-awareness* to pinpoint the conflicts and make the necessary adjustments to improve your circumstances.

As you work your way through this process, be sure to take your time and delve into the consequences of this change and how it could potentially impact your life, the lives of others and your circumstances. This is certainly not something that should be rushed. Rather, this is something that requires a lot of careful thought and attention.

Your very *first step* is to identify the unconscious drivers that you would like to change for yourself.

Ask yourself:

- What driver would I like to change? Describe it.

- How do I currently use my driver?

- In what specific situations do I use my driver?

- With whom do I use this driver?

- Why do I use this driver?

- How does this driver not serve me in these situations?

- Could it potentially serve me in certain situations and not in others?

- Does it provide me with any benefits that I would like to preserve?

Your unconscious driver may very well serve you in some way. There might actually be benefits that you will lose if you make these changes. As such, it's important for you to consider ways you could potentially preserve these benefits moving forward through this process.

Your next step is to pinpoint the unconscious driver that you would prefer to use instead.

Ask yourself:

- What driver would I like to use instead? Describe it.

- How and in what situations would I like to use this driver?

- How will this driver potentially serve me?

- What will it allow me to do? How is this of value?

Then test your new driver by simulating in your mind's eye. Imagine how you will use it in a variety of ways to help you attain your desired outcomes. Fully associate yourself within this experience using all of your sensory organs. While there, ask yourself:

- How does this driver feel?

- What does it look like?

- What does it seem like?

- What specific thoughts do I have about it?

- What does it feel like to use it daily?

- Do I feel excitement, satisfaction, discomfort, or pain?

As you work through these questions, picture yourself in different situations using this driver. It's important that this new driver serves you within these specific situations or else there might be conflicts. As a result, you will fail to make the necessary long-term changes.

Now it's time to step away from you and view this driver from an outsider's perspective, as an observer. No longer are you viewing this change from within yourself, but rather outside yourself. From this perspective ask yourself:

- What do I notice about myself?

- What do I notice about the changes that I am making?

- How are these changes affecting me?

- What will these changes allow me to do, to be, to experience, and to have?

- How do these changes affect or influence my current beliefs, values and convictions?

- What am I able to do as a result of these changes? Why is this important?

- What might I be no longer able to do as a result of these changes?

- How does this change affect me – my life – and others in the short and long-term?

- What are the positive and negative consequences of this change?

Having spent time outside of you, it's now time to step back inside yourself and ask yourself one more critical question:

- Does any part of me object to this change that I am about to make?

It's very possible that you might have conflicting beliefs, values and/or convictions. It might also be possible that the current driver actually serves you in some way. Your mind is now resisting this change, because you are about to lose something that has been serving you all this time. There's comfort in familiarity. Your brain's sole purpose is to help you survive, so it will resourcefully test a lot of the argument you put forward to yourself about change. It is essential to think about ways you can preserve the benefits of your current driver while changing to the new driver. Assess and address these *internal* conflicts and incongruities before continuing with this process.

One way you can address these conflicts and incongruities is to reframe your circumstances. Reframing involves shifting how you think about things in order to change how you feel about them. This will depend on your particular circumstances and does require some resourcefulness and insight.

You can, for instance, reframe your circumstances by:

- Offering counter examples
- Using a different story
- Redefining your experience
- Changing time frames

- Playing around with your perspectives

We talked extensively about reframing in Chapter 1.

Finally, make a conscious agreement with yourself that you will install this new unconscious driver. Remember that for the new driver to work, you must have the necessary desire, motivation and commitment to make positive and lasting change, working with it until it becomes a new habit that no longer requires any thought and attention. Without this commitment, motivation and desire, you will fail to follow through properly and will fall back into old patterns. The mind is very strong, so it's paramount that you practice this new driver in real life as well as in your imagination until it becomes comfortable and familiar. Only then will you develop the necessary momentum you need to make lasting change work for you in the long run.

CHAPTER 15
CREATE YOUR OWN IDENTITY

'Your identity is your most valuable possession. Protect it!'

WHO ARE YOU?

Be yourself!

Your identity or your personal brand is what differentiates you from other people. Your personal brand is your calling card; it's what you are known for and how others experience you. People with strong personal brands are very clear with who they are and what makes them stand out from the crowd.

Take a moment and answer the questions below:

- Who do you want to be?

_____

_____

- Who did you want to be when you were growing up?

_____

_____

- Who do you daydream of being?

_____

_____

Did you answer *you*?

You know, 98% of the time when people are asked the question *'who do you want to be?'* they say they want to be someone else! Don't feel bad if those thoughts were roaming around your head as you were reading, but stop. Delve a little deeper. *Why* don't you want to be *you*?

Usually, if you're thinking you might prefer to be someone else, it's a sure sign that there's something that you're avoiding dealing with. Something within yourself that you just don't want to face up to, or look at.

So, grab a pen and paper and ask yourself: What is it that I am not dealing with? See what comes to mind. Write everything down in a big burst; don't think too hard and let your unconscious mind run free.

Then you have a starting point for dealing with some of those things you've been ignoring. Which, you should know by now, are not going to go away (in fact, they will become stronger and stronger repeating patterns) unless you start to pay them some attention.

BUILDING YOUR PERSONAL BRAND

'If your presence doesn't make an impact, your absence won't make a difference.'

To build a strong personal brand, you must have a strong sense of *'self'* or know thy self. What are your key character traits? What are you good at? What are you passionate about? What do you value about yourself and what do others value about you?

Here's something to try:

Imagine for a moment that you are at a party with your friends and family. You step out of the room for a moment. If you were a fly on the wall, what would this group of people – your nearest and dearest – say about you?

Write them down.

_____
_____
_____

Now imagine you are at work with all your colleagues, supervisors and leaders. What do you think they would say about your personal brand? What kind of words would they use to describe you?

_____
_____
_____

Are they similar words from your personal to your professional list? There should be a few, because no matter what the environment, your personal brand will always shine through. Now choose one, something that resonates strongly. One beautiful word!

This is your personal brand.

Feedback is critical for improvement

> *'Good feedback is the key to improvement.'*

Now, it's time to gather some feedback. Go to your friends and family and do this exercise for you. Ask them for one word that describes who you are or what your personal brand means to them. Then you can do the same thing at work.

Tell people that you're inviting them to be honest, because the only way you will grow is uncovering how others perceive you or get insight into some of your unconscious drivers. Those blind spots I keep talking about.

Have a look at the common words that come up and think about why they did. Words like – committed, trustworthy, loyal, passionate or creative. Whatever word stands out is what you do better than anyone else. You will find that quite often people frequently compliment you or praise you on that very word.

You need to tap into that word, deep dive and look:

- How do you do what you do?
- What makes you achieve your results?
- What energises or ignites you?

Everyone has a personal brand, and often it's a matter of improving or reconstructing or tweaking our personal brand as we evolve through life. Knowing where to start is the key. Feedback can provide that starting point.

Being aware of ourselves in this way gives focus to our understanding of how we are perceived by others. Perhaps they think we are always late or always rushing. Perhaps they think we take too long to ponder decisions. Some of these perceptions can give us vital insight into the way we think, act and behave, because sometimes our actions are so deeply unconscious, we don't even know that we're doing them.

Measurement, evaluation and assessment

- Can you state your 6 most relevant and compelling personal brand attributes?

- What emotion do you display the most when things are going well?

- What emotion you display the most when things are in crisis mode?

- Do people feel open and comfortable with you? If not, then why not?

- Do you burn bridges easily when you leave a relationship or a job?

- What kind of situations or people do you attract most of the times?

- Do you attend functions where you know you will meet people that you need to know?

- Can you describe how you are different from your peers and why?

- Do you know how and when to end conversations comfortably?

- Do you find clever ways to re-connect and stay in touch with contacts?

- Can you state the 6 most relevant and compelling personal brand attributes if those around you were to say were your greatest strength?

- Do you know how your self-perceptions differ from the perceptions of those around you?

- Can you clearly describe the people who need to know about your brand more so that you can achieve your goals?

- What kind of personal and professional problems do people bring to you?

- What are your 6 strongest professional traits?

- Which of the 3 traits do you enjoy the most?

- What do you think is your most consistent trait?

- What trait do you need to change?

Taking the time to do this will help you to understand what key attributes make up your personal brand. What kind of character are *you* shaping out to be?

CREATING A DESIRE MAP

Once you have all of this wonderful insight, you can use it to create a desire map, which helps you figure out where you're at. It also provides some clues for getting to where you want to be.

But here's the thing. The journey is just as important as the destination, if not more so. So, be sure to give your desire map some authenticity – specifics are good, but don't stress yourself out by creating too many fixed points. Otherwise, you'll end up feeling stressed that you can't commit, or de-motivated when you don't meet a milestone. Chill out, and have fun with the process!

Personal Brand Perception	The meaning you give it	Personal Brand desire

List all the most common personal brand words that keep coming up for you – the things people say – in the first column. Take a look. What do they mean to you? Fill out your answers in the second column – the meaning you give it.

How far apart is your goal from where you are today to where you want to be? What new skills do you want to develop and which do you want to refine? Fill those answers in the last column – Personal Brand Desire.

This will help you create goals on what you need to do to get to where you want to get to. Assign dates to each task so that you are creating movement.

Your personal brand encompasses how you think, how you look, how you speak and how you behave. Most of these are unconscious and the only way to find out our blind spots is by asking those around us.

Again, ask your friends and family to contribute here. This can be a very empowering exercise, because most of the time many of us are very surprised at the way we are viewed by others. The image of ourselves that we carry around is so often negative, and this exercise will help you to see just how amazing, talented and unique you really are.

Ask them – how do you:

Think	Look	Speak	Behave
Visionary	*Elegant*	*Clearly*	*Composed*

TAKE YOUR IDENTITY OUT OF YOUR DECISIONS

> *"Your visions will become clear only when you can look into your own heart. Who looks outside, dreams; who looks inside, awakes."* –
> **C.G. Jung**

If 95% of our decisions are made by the unconscious mind, then the other 5% are made by the conscious mind.

Up until this moment, your personal brand has been all unconscious. This is the moment that you get to reshape it – to change your identity in a conscious manner.

This change is fundamental to all of the work that you've been undertaking in the previous chapters. It's inextricably linked with your environment and the people you spend time with.

DECLUTTER YOUR RELATIONSHIPS

Many of us keep friendships and relationships out of laziness, fear, or a shared sense of history (but little else in common), complacency and neediness. But just like our wardrobes, our shoe closets and our kitchens, our friendships need Spring Cleaning from time to time! We need to get rid of the *'clutter'* that no longer serves our best interests.

If the people around you light you up, energise you and support you, keep them. If they make you feel like you want to crawl under a bed and lie in the foetal position, then you need a plan of escape. This does not mean you have to be mean or rude or just cut people off, you can extract yourself with quiet dignity and – if you do it well – leave the other person feeling better for having known you, rather than sad that you're going to be no longer in contact.

Conscious design shapes your unconscious identity. If you're trying to shape your future and achieve certain outcomes, you'll get the most leverage from focusing on your identity. By using conscious decision-making to shape your identity, you can make conscious decisions that shape the new you!

The powerful question to ask is: *'Does it fit my new brand?'*

When you start to think like this, you begin to make decisions and take action and, eventually, this entire personal brand *'attributes'* will influence your choices and decisions consciously, until it becomes second nature.

> *"Whatever we plant in our unconscious mind and nourish with repetition and emotion will one day become a reality."* – **Earl Nightingale**

DIFFERENT ROLES WE PLAY

In life, we wear many hats and we play various roles. For example:

- Mother
- Wife
- Friend
- Auntie
- Cousin
- Daughter
- Husband
- Business owner
- Neighbour
- Father
- Brother
- Son
- Sister
- Uncle
- Customer
- Student

These roles shape our personal brand too. We've considered our roles as family members and co-workers and we solicited feedback to help us shape our personal brand, but to go deeper. It's important to explore these other roles too, and how they feed into our personal brand.

For instance, if you are a mother, you will:

- Want the best for your children
- Want them to be safe
- Perhaps be strict
- Want them to study hard

What are some of the most common words or lines you use as a mother?

- Are you feeling okay?
- How can I help you out?
- Don't forget to take your lunch!
- Tell me, what's wrong?

Also, it can be something completely different, like:

- Go and clean up your room!
- How many times do I need to repeat myself?
- Eat all your vegetables!
- Because I said so!

As a mother in this role, what kinds of feelings come up for you?

- Love
- Compassion
- Satisfaction
- Pride

Below create 6 circles. In each circle, write down the different roles you play out in your life and then fill the circles with:

- How you think
- What you say
- How you feel
- How you behave

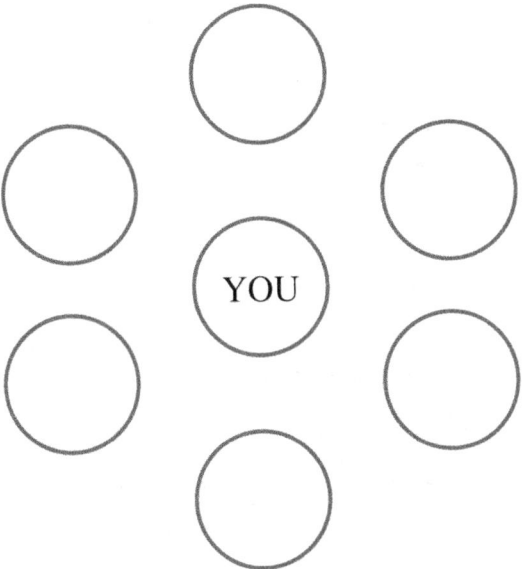

For example:

I am a mother

How you think – I am here to make sure my son is protected, happy, healthy and comfortable.

What you say – What have you eaten today?

How you feel – I am happy to see the man he has become.

How you behave – Over-protective, to the point where it may come across controlling. Not my intention of course, just a matter of love and caring.

I am a wife

How you think – I am blessed to have such a supportive loving partner.

What you say – What have you eaten today? And I love you.

How you feel – Happy to see him happy and free to do what he wants to do.

How you behave – Over-protective, to the point where it may come across controlling. Not my intention of course, just a matter of love and caring.

I am a business-owner

How you think – I want to make a difference and expose other individual personal powers.

What you say – You can do anything as long as you put your mind to it.

How you feel – I am extremely happy to see individuals go through self-realisation, growth and connect with their internal self.

How you behave – Giving them the space and freedom to come to their own realisations.

I am a sister

How you think – I am here to make sure my brother is protected, happy and comfortable.

What you say – What have you eaten today?

How you feel – Happy to see him happy and free.

How you behave – Over-protective, to the point where it may come across controlling. Not my intention of course, just a matter of love and caring.

I am a daughter

How you think – I am blessed to have an angel as a mother, so caring and giving; it's quite scary how much alike we are.

What you say – You should take care of your health. I am being selfish, but I want you here as long as possible.

How you feel – Worried about my mother's health and really want her to take health seriously, but we come from a different generation.

How you behave – Over-protective, to the point where it may come across controlling. Not my intention of course, just a matter of love and caring.

I am a coach

How you think – I am blessed that I do what I love most, which is to help people. I never have to work a day in my life.

What you say – What do you want to create for yourself? This world is your oyster and it is here for the taking.

How you feel – That everyone has all the answers and resources they require to get to their destiny, it's a matter of guiding them through the path.

How you behave – Optimistic, enthusiastic and positive that they will achieve exactly what they desire.

Roles	Positive	Negative

Families, friends and relationships shape who we are. What role do your family and friends play in establishing who you are?

Although we can't choose our family, we can choose to decide how we think about them, and how we behave around them to get the right results. So what actions are you going to start creating for yourself?

If we have friends, acquaintances or environments that are not conducive to our growth, then why stay where we are when we have a choice? Relationships teach us lessons, so what lesson have you learned and what do they mean to you? What have you learned about yourself?

With these kinds of experiences, we have to embrace them and not be afraid to challenge the status quo. Have you ever given up something that you really wanted to do and believe in – just because one of your connections said you couldn't do it?

Take time now to reflect on all of your work and create a mind map with you in the middle; map out all the factors that you feel challenged by and ones that have an impact on your identity. Write all your beliefs around these different roles you play out with these different characters, and write a short reflective piece on a person in your life who has challenged you the way you see the world. How have you changed as a result of your relationship with them?

Do you think the individual who you have been challenged with has a strong sense of self? If your response is no, then why give it another thought. If the answer is yes, then how can you use this to turn it into a positive growth mindset and as constructive feedback for change?

All relationships teach us great lessons. It's up to us whether we want to face them or not.

CONNECTION AND BELONGING

'Connection is the number one human need.'

It improves our physical health and psychological well-being. It may sound a little out there, but now there is research that shows a lack of social connection that leads to loneliness, which leads to other health problems such as obesity, anxiety and depression.

Conversely, research also shows us that a healthy social lifestyle has links to strong immune systems and longevity. Of course, there are also those famous stories about how Australian soldiers endured prison camps and other atrocities during World War I and II by having a strong sense of *'mate-ship'*, a shared sense of belonging and connection which helped them to remain optimistic, even in adversity.

Added to this, there are studies of children in orphanages around the world that document that children who are touched and hugged have less illness and better survival rates than children who do not have physical contact with their volunteer carers.

Connection to others provides us with:

- a higher rate of self-esteem
- a higher rate of empathy
- a higher rate of trust
- a lower rate of depression
- a lower rate of sadness
- a lower rate of anxiety

> *"Those who have a strong sense of love and belonging have the courage to be imperfect."* – **Brené Brown**

Biologically, we are wired to connect and belong. Our brain seeks safety. When we feel like we belong – physically, emotionally and mentally – we feel safe. This support gives us the courage to take risks. When we take risks, we can stretch, grow and evolve.

Belonging and connecting gives us a greater ability to co-operate too. When we have this sense of being part of a *'tribe'*, we have a greater sense that we can make a difference and that we are contributing to a greater good.

Attachment vs. Connection

Attachment and Connection are very different.

Attachment doesn't have to be reciprocal. Attachment can lead to pain and suffering, possession or obsession. It can leave you feeling needy and guilty and it diminishes your personal power.

Connection is a two-way flow of energy between 2 individuals who understand they are part of a greater whole. It is characterised by mutual energy, cooperation, collaboration and communication.

So why do we get attached to ideas, places, people and things?

Attachment is an emotional dependence that we put on ideas, places, people or things we *want*, we *wish*, we *need*, and it leads to pain and suffering because we are always thinking that this very thing is the thing that is going to make us different, happy, content, fulfilled. And when we get it, it makes us feel terrific for a while. But, because of the very nature of this universe we live in – everything is impermanent – when that thing or person changes or leaves, we end up feeling sad, angry, lonely, and upset.

See how this can lead to pain and suffering? The power here is to practice non-attachment and letting go.

Living with non-attachment sounds easier than it really is, but it is the very thing that will get you everything you want! Be clear of the end goal, but don't be attached to it. It's tricky.

> *"Can you step back from your own mind and thus understand all things? Giving birth and nourishing, having without possessing, acting with no expectations, leading and not trying to control: this is the supreme virtue."* – **Lao Tzu**

By living a life of non-attachment, you allow the freedom of the outcome rather than the control of the outcome. By trying to control it all, we often exclude ourselves from glorious opportunities. Things come and go in life and that is the cycle of our experience and lesson. You can love greatly without attachment, but you can have strong connection, which is a very different energy indeed.

THE IMPACT OF INFLUENCE

> *"The people who influence you are the people who believe in you"* – **Henry Drummond**

There is very little that we do in this life that does not involve other people. Healthy relationships thrive on a mutual exchange of energy.

To achieve this, not only do you need to understand what special qualities those people who influence us have, but also in turn, what special qualities we have which make us influence them.

In order to have balance, which is critical, we each need to understand our exchange value. This is also known as the *law of reciprocity*, which means to give and take mutually, to return in kind.

To use this in your own life, you need to change your mindset by assuming that *everyone* can help you. Then you need to be very clear about what you can barter or exchange – what you can offer in return to make the relationship mutually beneficial. Sometimes, this is not always apparent at first.

You also need to be clear about your reasons for wanting to influence another – what's the goal? (Your desired outcome). Then you need to understand the other person's world…what's important to them? How can you influence?

It's also important to remember that in everything we do, there is a *cost* and a *benefit*. The potential *cost* of a relationship is those things that we see as negative, being annoying, controlling or needy. The rewards or *benefits* of a relationship are those aspects that we see as positive, giving, supporting, nurturing, communicative, and how we feel when we are with this person. This cost-benefit analysis can help us keep track of our net rewards and the overall value of the relationship. (This was also explored in Chapter 9 when we discussed the Relationship Trust Account).

Our attitudes have an impact on our behaviours.

Attitude – what are they like?	**Behaviour** – what are they doing?
Pessimistic	Always sees the negative in everything
Arrogant	Always interrupts when I'm talking
Secretive	Doesn't ever give me all the information
Angry	Always snaps at me
Doubtful	Indecisive all the time and hesitates to do anything

Imagine that your partner is *pessimistic* all the time – what are the *costs* and *benefits* to the relationship of this attitude?

Cost	Benefit
They don't interact well with friends	They get to do their own thing
They don't trust anyone	They don't have to open up about their feelings
They never want to try new things	They get to go to their same places all the time

Now it's your turn to give it a go. By doing this, it will give you a great understanding of the other person's situation and what seems to be important for this individual.

Cost	Benefit

It's impossible to change people. But if you can be certain about what matters to you and what matters to them, then you can develop a healthy exchange of energy and a mutual bartering can take place – this is the foundation of healthy relationships. Tolerance and acceptance are paramount of ourselves and of others.

Alan Cohen and *David Bradford* identified 5 types of currencies that we, as humans, value highly.

Inspiration. To influence people who value inspiration, you need to appeal to their passion, goals and sense of purpose or the contribution they can make to a valued cause.

Task. More often than not, this relates to *'ticking it off the list'*, getting something completed and having the satisfaction of doing so. Often the exchange here would be money, personnel or supplies.

Position. This relates to recognition, reputation and visibility. People who value this currency are usually highly motivated and want to get ahead. They also want to be recognised and rewarded.

Relationship. These people are often driven by feelings and connections with other people. They value belonging – emotional support and understanding. Show these individuals gratitude.

Personal. These individuals are driven by personal needs and wants. By showing them sincere gratitude for their help and allowing them the freedom to make their own decisions as they are focused on their needs. Keep things simple for them, so they don't feel hassled helping you.

What are your relevant exchanges?

- Recognition
- Power
- Control
- Ownership
- Security
- Awareness

If you assume that everyone is a potential ally, people actually want to help you, and you are opening up a healthy exchange by giving them an opportunity to do so, then limitless possibilities open up to you. By understanding how you can influence that person and conduct a mutually beneficial exchange, you can develop relationships that have appropriate boundaries and which are founded on mutual give and take.

The exercise here is to look at the most influential people in your life, those closest to you. Can you figure out what your exchange values are?

Your exchange	Their exchange

Now that you have analysed the relationship, you should have a good insight into the other person. So...we now make the exchange.

What are we going to exchange?

This for	That

A *win-win* attitude changes the way you think, feel and behave. You will seek benefits for both people and your relationships will no longer be one-sided with one person relying on the other. This kind of co-dependency is so draining and it can't last. You're on a path to be your very best self, so surround yourself with relationships that allow you to be just that.

Embracing vulnerability

> *"In total surrender of the ego, the transformation of our vibration unfolds by itself, to levels far beyond our imagination"* – **Annette Duveroth**

When going through this exercise, you may experience that your *'stuff'* comes up. This is totally normal. You may find yourself in a state of being vulnerable for the outcome to be a win-win situation. But there is *strength* in embracing your vulnerability, which allows you to create a stronger connection with people.

When you connect from the heart, you are standing in your truth. You can let go of the need to be strong, surrender to your vulnerability and watch miracles happen. Connection gives us *purpose* and *meaning*. Some people see vulnerability as a sign of weakness, but it's quite the opposite. There is great strength in being vulnerable.

When others speak to you about their *vulnerability* or *fears,* don't you find that this helps to dissolve the barriers and opens you up to respond gently, carefully, and from a place of compassion and empathy? If all exchanges could be this way, the world would be a vastly different place!

Vulnerability is a natural state for human beings – we are born into the world this way – very dependent upon others for our care and survival.

But as adults, both surrender and vulnerability are uncertain territories. There is a level of risk involved in opening up to these. In fact, the simple act of *'opening up'* is surrender, letting go and allowing your vulnerability to shine.

Vulnerability is the doorway to knowing, becoming aware of and surrendering to your true self. This awareness is a step towards *freedom*.

To surrender is not about giving up; it's about letting go of all attachments and trusting the process of life.

> *"Surrender to what is. Let go of what was. Have faith in what will be."* – **Sonia Ricotti**

Change is the essence of life, so be willing to surrender who you are for what you could become – your true identity!

CHAPTER 16
MANIFESTING ABUNDANCE

"Imagination is everything. It is a preview for life's coming attraction" – **Albert Einstein**

WEALTH CREATION

Wherever I go, I am attracting wealth and prosperity in unlimited abundance!

This is not the first time you will have heard of the idea of manifesting, the concept of being able to bring into your life everything that you desire, no matter what it is.

People who understand how manifesting works, and who practice it on a regular basis will tell you that it's for real; not voodoo.

To understand the idea of manifesting is to understand the *law of attraction:* the premise that *like attracts like*. Essentially, this means that if you think negatively, that's what you'll attract. But by thinking positively, positive things are what you will receive.

In Chapter 1, we discovered that *thoughts are powerful things*. To recap, if we *think* a certain way, this is what we will *see*, then this is how we *behave*, so this is what you *feel* and the *result* will be exactly what you *get*. Whatever you feel, positive or negative, you are going to attract exactly that!

It is that simple, we human beings just have a tendency to make it complex.

So, if you *believe* that you have an *abundance* of *wealth,* and that all you have to do is act and live as if you already have it, then it is coming your way.

Remember what the great Henry Ford said – *"Whether you think you can or think you can't, you're right!"*

In addition to that, I would *always* be conscious about how I desire or want something that I haven't got in my possession. Let me give you an example, have you ever desired something like a new watch, Fitbit or car? When you had these strong emotions attached to your desire (fuelling your desire), what happened? Did you lose the item? Did you have an accident or your car broke down?

You see, the moment you have a strong desire, you are sending a message out to the universe and as the saying goes, *"ask and you shall receive"*. All you need to do the next time you have a *'desire'* is to make sure you complete your desire with:

- I will have this item when I choose it is the right time
- I desire this item in the understanding that there will be no loss or damage to my existing item
- As long as my desire doesn't harm anyone or anything in the process

You are not a physical being in a physical universe. You are a *vibrational* being in a vibrational universe. You are both a *transmitter* and a *receiver* of energy. One of our greatest challenge as a human being is learning how to live as a vibrational being in a vibrational universe. To be able to shift your vibration and manifest your desire, you have to think of yourself as a vibrational *transmitter*. You are constantly sending out signals that tell the universe who you are – at that very moment and those signals will attract certain vibrational beings and experiences into your life.

In other words, if your energy radiates *wealth* and *abundance* then guess what? Your physical reality will reflect wealth and abundance for your physical being. As soon as you can accept that your vibrational self attracts compatible patterns, it becomes more apparent that if you want to experience something different in your life, you must somehow change the signals you are putting out. And the only way to do that is to quiet your mind and tune into your inner being and listen to the ever broadcasting radio station that is YOU! So what types of signals are you broadcasting?

UNCONSCIOUS MONEY BLOCKS

Money is energy. It is a means of exchange for your goods or service. The money you receive for that work balances the energy that you put into your work.

But some of us have unconscious *money blocks* that we are not even aware of and these stop us from truly getting what we want.

What are money blocks?

Money blocks are limiting beliefs that you have about money. Money blocks are unconscious beliefs and you are probably not aware of them. They may be having a massive impact in your life or business.

Where do they come from?

They are old programs that were ingrained or imposed in some way, shape or form from your upbringing. That could be from what you saw on TV, what you heard at school or maybe some sayings from your parents when they were teaching you the value of money with comments like – *'money doesn't grow on trees'* or *'money is evil'*. Even if you grew up seeing your parents always fighting about money, your unconscious mind will have this belief that money causes arguments.

Here are some money blocks that you may relate to.

Self-worth – *Receiving money.* Believe it or not, some of us feel very uncomfortable about *receiving money*. If you have low self-worth, if you are someone who will put everyone else's needs ahead of your own, then the message that you're sending out is that you only need enough money for everyone else and your own needs can wait. So, this is exactly what will keep happening over and over again until you consciously change that unconscious behaviour. This kind of behaviour leads to not asking for a pay raise or working longer hours than you are paid for.

> *"The most delightful surprise in life is to suddenly recognise your own worth."* – **Maxwell Maltz**

Self-sabotage – *Having money*. Some people feel uncomfortable about *having money*, so they spend it. Is this you? As soon as it comes into the bank account, do you spend it on impulsive shopping sprees, buying all sorts of things you don't need? This kind of behaviour leads to feeling insecure about money because it cannot be saved.

> *"Be careful how you are talking to yourself because you are listening."* – **Lisa M. Hayes**

Self-evaluation – *Comparison*. Some people just can't help themselves, and they are constantly comparing their situation with everyone else. This type of thinking is just perpetuating exhaustion because there is never a happy ending. It goes on and on and on because you are always seeking external gratification or validation. This is deeply rooted in your self-worth and it will continually show up in your financial worth. It can lead to feeling like a victim, with everyone else to blame. The truth is that you are unique. You have gifts and talents. Why not focus on them, instead of giving your power away?

> *"Comparison is the thief of joy."* – **Theodore Roosevelt**

Friends – *Influence*. Basically, our friends have a huge influence over how we feel, think and behave. This is what is called the *collective sum* of the conscious of the people you are with. These combined will give you a weighted impact on who you become. When it comes to relationships, we are greatly influenced, whether we like it or not. It's our self-esteem and our decision-making where we are more affected by our environment than we think, especially when people around us have a *success* or a *poverty* consciousness.

> *"You are the average of the five people you spend the most time with."* – **Jim Rohn**

Exchange – *You have to give to receive*. The law of circulation states that all things in the universe are always flowing in circulation but at an ever-expanding rate. Some of us are in business and have to negotiate prices for our goods and services, negotiating a price can be daunting to some. The important thing to remember is the circulation – what goes around comes around. You can have all the money that you want in life, but you have to be willing to give too, and help others to get what they want with your services that will add value to them.

> *"If you would take, you must first give; this is the beginning of intelligence."* – **Lao Tzu**

Perception – *Stories*. We all have stories about money. Maybe you experienced your parents *fighting about money*, so now you think money is evil. This kind of money block is related to *negative emotions* such as shame, fear, grief, guilt or anger, which are all unconscious and can be re-engineered to make way for more positive associations with money.

> *"Your perception of me is a reflection of you; my reaction to you is an awareness of me."* – **Anonymous**

Releasing money blocks

Before removing all of our *money blocks* and continuing this chapter, we first have to become aware of what they are by tapping into the power or our unconscious mind – receiving the abundance of money that is our birthright.

Releasing any money block is having *clarity* over what it is. Once you can verbalise your money block and how it personally applies to you, it stops having as much power over you.

Can you relate to any of the above money blocks? Which ones? Write down exactly how and why you can relate to them.

Now what can you do to release them? Name 12 things that you can do to release your money blocks.

From 1 to 10, how committed are you to making those changes? Anything that is 5 and under, there is not enough motivation or drive to break-through your money block.

If you are having trouble breaking through your money blocks, lets deep dive and work on it together.

Let's say your money block is *Self-sabotage*, it would go like this.

- **Unconscious belief** – saving money is way too hard
- **Unconscious thinking** – I am not good at saving money
- **Unconscious behaviour** – impulsive buying clothes, jewellery or furniture that you don't need
- **Results** – never have enough money to pay for my bills or credit card

Now we can turn that around by focusing on it for 21 one days consciously.

- **Conscious belief** – Saving money is easy and necessary
- **Conscious thinking** – I am good at saving money
- **Conscious behaviour** – I open up a savings account that takes $100 a week out of my pay
- **Results** – My bank balance is increasing, making me feel confident about having enough money.

Now you try it:

Unconscious belief

Unconscious thinking

Unconscious behaviour

Results

Transform from unconscious to conscious.

Conscious belief

Conscious thinking

Conscious behaviour

Results

You can eliminate your *money blocks* by spending time on <u>you</u>. Clear them all step by step until they become less and less of an obstacle for you.

This is the secret of getting everything we want out of life. We attract whatever we choose to give our attention to, whether wanted or unwanted. So remember, if you continue to focus on the *lack and limitation* in your life, you will continue to create and attract more lack and limitation. Instead, if you focus on the *wealth, abundance* and *prosperity* that are already present in your life, no matter how small, then you will begin to create and attract more wealth, abundance and prosperity.

Even if it doesn't exist in your life, act as if you already have it. Remember, the mind can't tell the difference between what is real or not real, so fake it until you make it!

SUCCESS VS. POVERTY CONSCIOUSNESS

For example, someone who has a success consciousness will have an attitude of:

- Hope
- Enthusiasm
- Compassion
- Non-judgmental
- Kindness
- Generosity
- Selfless

- Accepting of others (strengths and weaknesses)
- Focused
- Being valued
- Prosperous
- Fortunate

All in all, they see that fulfilling others needs is the key to success.

However, one that has a poverty consciousness will have an attitude of:

- Critical
- Negative (pessimist)
- Selfish
- Feeling not worthy of success
- Pay me more for less work
- That's not my department
- We can't do that
- This will never work
- That's not my job
- Not giving to others (emotionally)
- Not sharing with others
- Laziness
- Being a victim of circumstance and blame the world
- Seek out other poverty-conscious people to reinforce and be reinforced

As you can see, a success mindset or consciousness will allow for more opportunity, more flow, more success.

Friends impact upon us collectively and can have an effect on our thinking, behaviour and actions.

These personalities may or may not be aligned with who you are today, yet we put up with them and keep them in our lives even though they are no longer aligned to our values and principles. This is what is called the *collective sum* of the conscious of our friends. What are they in your group of friends? Or even at work and how do they influence you?

This collective of personalities will be made up of many complex facets, but often the pursuit of opportunity can be simplified and boiled right down to a *success* or *poverty* consciousness.

To put it into an example, if 2 different people were given the same situation, one would focus on the positive side of what can be accomplished and the other on the negative side. Both of these individuals would reap the results that reflect what energy vibration they give out upon their focus towards the event experienced. Even though you certainly know what the desired outcome is, what you focus upon determines what you get.

It is how we choose to look at it.

So how do you get yourself from poverty consciousness to success consciousness?

First, catch your *thinking* in time. Don't allow going down the road of poverty consciousness. Then *listening* to your words and start to change your conversations – shift from using negative language to using more positive language, like we did in Chapter 4.

Look for ways to become more proactive and co-operative. Start searching for methods to create more opportunities by inviting people to look at possibilities. By shifting your focus, you will move into success consciousness and you will help create a more pleasant and healthier environment for everyone involved.

"Every failure brings with it the seed of an equivalent success." –
Napoleon Hill

Remember, there is no such thing as failure, there is only feedback, so keep going.

GRATITUDE AND APPRECIATION

"Gratitude turns what you have into enough." – **Buddha**

Consistent *gratitude* and *appreciation* is an easy way to ending poverty consciousness. When your abundance is measured by how deeply you *feel* abundant and how often you visit this feeling, then your experience of being *wealthy* is truly unstoppable. This is the most direct path to attract and magnetise financial freedom fast and abundantly to you in your outer world.

Gratitude is an appreciation of what you have; it is magnetic. The more *gratitude* you have, the more *abundance* you will attract.

Gratitude opens doors. To cultivate the habit of being grateful, you need to make a list so that you show gratitude, appreciation and thankfulness.

What are you grateful for today? Write down as many things that come to mind.

Talents	People	Material Objects

Now take time to reflect on each thing that you are grateful for and write down *why* you are grateful.

_____
_____
_____
_____
_____
_____

To make your list come to life, write down a thank you letter, card or email to the people that you are grateful to have in your life, how they help you and how they make your life better. Be honest and sincere.

There is no point having these amazing people in your life if you can't share how you feel for them.

Don't forget to be grateful for the everyday things like being alive, having a roof over your head and food on the table. Appreciate the simple things in life like a park or a beach.

If you practice to find the good in every experience – even the negative experiences, as they lead us to opportunities – you will build and improve your gratitude, allowing bigger and better things to come into your life. This is the cure to poverty consciousness in a nutshell!

So, now that we have removed all money blocks and poverty consciousness, we now have a positive mental attitude and are filled with enthusiasm. How do we manifest abundance, wealth and prosperity?

You have to be very clear of <u>what</u> exactly you want:

- What do you desire?

_____

_____

- For what purpose?

_____

_____

AUTOSUGGESTIONS AND AFFIRMATIONS

'I now live, feel and expect an abundance of money.'

Autosuggestions and affirmations are short and powerful statements. To affirm means to say something positive; it means to declare firmly and assert something to be true. By repeating an affirmation daily for 21 days, you can turn your affirmations into your unconscious thoughts.

As we discussed in many places during the course of this book, our negative thinking can be exceptionally powerful. Affirmations are tools that make us consciously aware of our thoughts. When you start making conscious positive thoughts, you actually become more aware of the negative thoughts that are always threatening to take over.

Be careful of what you think, because what you think is what you get. Create what you think about instead because as you think a certain thought, your brain produces chemicals that cause you to feel exactly the way you are thinking. Once you feel the way you think, you begin to think the way you feel and this goes on and on creating a feedback loop creating a state of *'being'*.

Affirmations are statements where you assert that what you want to be true is true.

Let's give it a go, shall we?

Going back to what you desire and for what purpose – let's say you desire <u>more money</u> and your purpose is <u>freedom.</u>

Examples of money affirmations:

- I am a magnet for money
- Prosperity is drawn to me
- Money comes to me in expected and unexpected ways
- I am worthy of making more money
- I embrace new avenues of income
- Money comes to me easily and effortlessly
- Wealth constantly flows into my life
- My actions create constant prosperity
- I am aligned with the energy of abundance
- I constantly attract opportunities
- I am the master of my wealth

Make it short and punchy!

Now that it is clear in your mind of what you want to create and you have an affirmation speaking as if you already have it, what are you going to give in return or as an exchange? My husband taught me an amazing technique – that when you really want something, what are you prepared to give up or sacrifice for what you want so badly? For example, when our little dog Seth had a stroke, we both gave up dark chocolate so that he would make it through and when the time comes for him to make his transition; we are having a chocolate party.

Energy is never lost, it is only transformed. Remember, there is no such thing as *something for nothing*. Even if it's time or privacy as your exchange, that is what you will commit to. So, what are you going to give up?

In our next chapter, we will go through goal setting and planning, but it's very important to have a date to when you want to achieve what you are affirming. So, give it a date now.

You have to believe it and have faith that it will manifest. The best way to do that is to repeat your affirmations daily – make it a habit. Here is how you do it.

1. Write your affirmation on a sticky note or make some really nice cards and get them laminated. Make them your own. Put

your energy, heart and feelings into your affirmation cards when writing them down.
2. If you used sticky notes, you can place them anywhere – in the car, in the bathroom, in your walk-in wardrobe – and everywhere.
3. Commit daily, 12 times a day, for 21 days. Read aloud 4 times in the morning, in the afternoon and the evening.
4. Relax before reading your affirmations so that you give it your 150% attention and focus. You don't want to be saying them out loud while you are running around getting ready for work. The more energy you give it, the more you will get back.
5. When you read your affirmations, you need to see it in your mind's eye and, most importantly, *feel* it. Adding immense emotion into it is like adding fuel to your car; it gives it power and distance.
6. The more you create your mental image, the more powerful it will become. Keep going and never give up!

You don't want to give up now only to find out later you were a meter away from gold!

3 KEYS TO SUCCESS AND WEALTH

> *Have you ever wondered what makes individuals, entrepreneurs and businesses successful?*

Do you think it's luck, circumstance or timings, brains or guts?

It's not any of these.

You might be surprised to find out what the real keys are.

Being comfortable with being uncomfortable

Human beings are creatures of habit, and we like to have some control over what happens next, so we're usually drawn to routine and reliability.

But, if we want to grow, change, evolve, transform, then we need to face challenges that expand our boundaries. This kind of instability helps us to understand exactly what we're capable of and learn more about ourselves in the process.

Successful people are always challenging themselves. They understand that when things become repetitive, predictable and ordinary, our expectations also drop and we no longer live a life that's bold, brave and exciting! Ironically, in trying to protect ourselves from the unknown, we virtually lose sight of the future. Then, we get stuck in perpetuating a mundane world – a world that might be safe, but is far from stimulating.

Testing your own limitations can be as simple as making a deal with yourself that you'll try something new. You'll soon discover that when you take yourself out of your comfort zone, marvellous things can happen!

An easy way to form new habits and to break old ones is to set an intention for 21 days. This helps you to create the discipline required to commit to change.

So, if you were to place yourself out of your comfort zone every day for 21 days, then you might be surprised by your tolerance. The more you practice being in a state of *'discomfort'*, the more adept you become at coping with it. New confidence will grow and you will see yourself evolving into a better version of yourself! If you can be comfortable with being uncomfortable, you will be prepared to handle whatever situation comes along in your own life.

Relevance

Relevance means being connected to the matter at hand. Why is *relevance* important? Because it focuses on results! *Relevance* is about achieving the desired goal. To understand your own *relevance*, you need to ask yourself:

- What's my purpose in life?
- Who am I (what do I stand for)?
- Why am I here?

This is a bit like defining your Vision and a Mission statement for yourself. Most people don't have either, which means they have no real clarity when it comes to defining what they are aiming to achieve in life. This, in turn, means that most of us are running around expending energy on all sorts of things that *don't matter*. But can you imagine how much more powerful, constructive and productive we can be, if we have a single-minded focus on the things that *do matter*?

Having clear goals helps to map out a path so that you can keep moving forward, advancing the way you want to live.

You might be one of those people who don't like too much structure in your life and the whole idea of goal setting is just *'blech'*. I'm here to tell you this is exactly why you should set goals. Because if you're really flexible, then you're also possibly easily distracted; goals keep you focused.

Furthermore, refer to point one: If you're not in the habit of goal setting, then it's out of your comfort zone and therefore something that's bound to be good for you on your quest for success.

Back to the point-at-hand. Whether you want business success, personal success or both, you must stay *relevant*. Essentially, this means that you must continue to reinvent yourself or your brand to ensure that you are at the forefront of people's minds. The consequence of not staying *relevant* is that people will not think of you and you will be left behind.

One simple way that you can ensure relevance and remind yourself to concentrate on it is to set yourself an intention throughout the day, especially if you feel that your energy is being distracted. Ask yourself: *'Is what I am doing right now relevant to my work or company?'*; *'Am I making a difference with what I am doing right now?'*; *'Is what I am doing moving me towards my goals?'*

With this focus, the right attitude and the right mindset, you will produce quality work that makes a difference.

Stay *relevant*! Focus on your authentic self, and the rest will fall into place.

Accountability

There is *no room for excuses*!

When you're fully accountable for your actions, you find out what you're really capable of. You make mistakes, you own those mistakes and you learn from them.

Accountability builds responsibility, *trust* and *respect*. These are big words in anyone's language.

When you are personally accountable, you take ownership of your actions and choices. If you are a leader, then your accountability extends beyond your own actions. You don't blame others when things go wrong. Instead, you go out of your way to make things right. It's also a fact that those leaders who take personal accountability have better social interactions with all relationships (their employees and clients) because their accountability builds trust and respect.

Someone who continually makes good on his or her promises and commitments is considered dependable and responsible. What follows is all kinds of good karma, like team members who will go the *'extra mile'* and clients who will come back again and again.

As we spoke about earlier in this book, *accountability* is not something that is automatic or comes naturally for some people, but it can become an acquired skill. Additional tips to become more personally accountable include:

- Don't say *yes* to everything. Manage your time and resources wisely. Things will fall through the cracks if you over-commit.
- Watch out for procrastination. This is a sign you are avoiding dealing with the problem. As soon as you find yourself procrastinating, stop and check in with your priorities. You'll probably find that the very thing you're procrastinating about is exactly what you should be focused on.

Ask for feedback:

- *What am I doing right?*
- *What opportunities for improvement do you see for me?*
- *What can I do differently?*

We all have the potential to be hugely successful. By following the 3 pillars for personal and business success, we can achieve great things. It just takes is a little courage, a little effort and a little understanding.

You are *responsible* and *accountable* for every aspect of your life. Yes, that's right. You are responsible means anything that comes into your life in the form of people, situation or circumstances – you are responsible for it! You are responsible for the movement that takes place inside of you in the form of thoughts, emotions and energy.

Accountable means you are accountable for all the change you wish to see in your life, be it with the outside situation, people or circumstances of your life. The easiest way to be *responsible* and *accountable* for everything that happens in your life is to stay aware in the present moment all the time.

'Ask and you shall receive' plays out all the time. Think about it. What question did you ask to have this life you are living as your answer? The life you are living right now is your path (response) to this question. So, what question did you ask? Look at your life and your path to see the question you have asked.

CHAPTER 17
YOUR JOURNEY OF TRANSFORMATION

'The greatest gift that you can give yourself is making time for yourself – your greatest asset.'

You are now on a journey of transformation. You are exploring the wisdom of your purpose. You are shedding old beliefs and stories that no longer fit who you are becoming. Stand in your truth, and get ready for an adventure of your authentic path.

When the world as we know it is no longer fulfilling or endurable, when there is a crisis, or when a door closes and we are *'called forth'* to step into a higher purpose, when the call rings up the curtain, when the familiar life horizon has been outgrown; the old concepts, ideals, and emotional patterns no longer fit; the time for passing the threshold is at hand.

You are now ready to tap into your prosperous life.

If right now you feel called to something greater than what your current job or life offers, you are ready to commence on your adventure and embark on your *Journey of Transformation*.

Stepping into the unknown to find your calling or to answer a call may involve:

- Facing fear of the unknown, uncertainty or obstacles
- Finding gold (your true self) – and your transforming idea
- Integrating your vision into your life and work

If you are undergoing a critical change in your life, such as wanting a career change, finding a meaningful relationship or recovering your creativity, you need to have a plan!

You must plan your work and work your plan.

> *"Your achievements can only be as good as the plans you make. If you fail to plan, you had better plan to fail."* – **Napoleon Hill**

PLANNING YOUR WORST CASE SCENARIO

Here's a tip. Before you delve into any new projects or goals, look at your best-case scenario and your worst-case scenario. If you can comfortably live with your worst-case scenario and you have a good backup plan, then there is no room for failure.

Best Case Scenario	Worst Case Scenario
I have lost 5 kg	I invested $5,000 on a well-being coach
My business is a success	I have to get a job
My liver is cleansed and healthy	I had to give up cheese and alcohol
I saved my relationship	I invested $5,000 in counselling

Now you give it a go!

Best Case Scenario	Worst Case Scenario

SMARTIE GOALS

To have a *plan* doesn't mean you have to have a 22-page plan. We are talking about a one-page, a simple plan. How I like to start my plan is by using **SMARTIE:**

- S   Specific (Significant)
- M   Measurable (Meaningful)
- A   Achievable (Action-Oriented)
- R   Relevant (Rewarding)
- T   Timely (Trackable)

I   Innovative (Creative Thinking)

E   Emotional (Connection)

From working through this book, I am sure by now you have a very clear idea of what you want to work on and I am sure you are crystal clear about what it is that you want to manifest for you!

What is the one thing that you want to achieve right now?

If that creates confusion, what I do is write a list of what I want to create for myself and then prioritise them in order of preference. When you have several goals, give each a priority. This helps you to avoid feeling overwhelmed by having too many goals, and helps to direct your attention to the most important ones. For the purpose of this exercise, you must only choose one for now.

But first, you have to know what you want.

- **S** – Specific: Keep your goal simple and focused, rather than wordy and vague. Be very specific about the outcome of what you want (who, what, where and why).
- **M** – Measurable: How will you know when you have reached your goal? What will be different? Can you track the progress of your goal?
- **A** – Achievable: Is your goal within your reach? Do you have the right resources, skill and knowledge to achieve this goal?
- **R** – Relevant: Is your goal worthwhile and is it relevant to your life's purpose?
- **T** – Timely: Set a date to your goal. This creates movement and movement is energy. Without the momentum of energy, nothing is possible.
- **I** – Innovative: Does your goal spark creativity? Does this new goal inspire a new way of thinking, feeling and behaviour?
- **E** – Emotion: What feelings do you connect with your goal? Does your goal excite you?

S _____
M _____
A _____
R _____
T _____
I _____
E _____

State your goal as if it's already been achieved, using positive and *'moving towards'* language. This trains the unconscious mind to accept the goal as real, which helps you stay motivated and focused.

Now write a statement using all of this information.

My Statement

_____
_____
_____
_____
_____
_____

Example Statement

It is the 22nd of December 2013; I am excited and I feel inspired to have lost 5 kg. I feel healthier and have an abundance of energy. I exercise 3 times a week and do yoga once a week. My weekly session with my Wellbeing coach inspires me every day to be my best me!

Now we need to create milestones. Milestones mark significant stages along the road to achieving your end goal. Create milestones easily by starting at the end (the accomplishment of the goal), and working your way backwards to your present day and circumstances.

Having milestones can help you stay on track by breaking your goal into smaller, tangible, so that you don't need to wait until you have completed your goal to feel like you have accomplished something along the way. If you are feeling overwhelmed by a large task, you can help ease your anxiety and make it feel more doable by breaking it down into smaller, more manageable chunks.

Try not to leave too much time or too little time between milestones.

For the purpose of this example, I am going to set weekly tasks. Let's say today is the 22nd of June 2013 and you have set your time as the 22nd of December to achieve your goal.

22nd June

22nd August

22nd September

22nd October

22nd November

_____

_____

_____

22nd December – Goal achieved!

Once you have done that, all you need to do is to complete your plan by making a list of tasks, with timelines that you need to complete in order to hit your milestones. Putting timelines on all of your tasks will create movement and builds up on your enthusiasm and motivation.

To finalise your plan, you need to make it visual. Remember, if you are going to engage with your unconscious mind, you need to speak the same language – pictures.

Make it *big*, you can be as creative as you like. I like to put it up on my wall with beautiful coloured paper. You can also invest in a weekly planner to help you out mapping your goals.

Block out all of your specific tasks in your calendar in advance so that you make the time to invest in your plan. Blocking out your time, helps you get a more realistic idea of how much time you actually have in a day, and don't forget to schedule in some time for you to disconnect! This is critical because once you get *'in the flow'*; it's easy to forget to *'switch off'*.

Planning makes the most of your time.

A goal without a plan is just a wish. Success doesn't happen if it's not planned for, so go ahead set your intentions for the week ahead and watch your life transform before your eyes.

CHANGE RESISTANCE INTO RESILIENCE

Everyone responds very differently to change – some thrive on change, some hate change and some are not fussed about change. As you go through your transformational journey, you may experience some resistance, which is quite normal when you consider we are creatures of habit. If you have been doing a certain thing for a decade, you will go through a process of change that is quite normal.

The number one reason why individuals resist change is because there is a *loss* in some way shape or form. For example, when you go through a change, you may lose your:

- Autonomy
- Security
- Status
- Purpose
- Identity
- People
- Certainty
- Responsibility
- Location
- Connection
- Friends
- Money

And...the list goes on. So, when you feel *resistance*, ask yourself – *'what is it that I am losing right now?'* You fear the loss of what?

When you feel resistance to change, you may experience:

- Fear of the unknown
- Connected to the old way
- Changes to routine

Maybe the reason why you may be feeling *resistance* could be as simple as you not having positive thoughts about you and your ability. Sometimes you may feel like you are losing control because you are going through an emotional roller coaster.

Master your *resistance* to become more *resilient*. What can influence your perspective on change is to understand the *what, when* and *why* and, of course, your instinctive response to change. For example, your previous experience with change and how many times you have done it before. All play a role in how you become *resilient* to change.

When you see change for what it is – *change* is about moving from the present (something that is known and familiar) through a *transition*, to something that is new, unfamiliar and in the future.

What is the difference between change and transition?

Change is an external event; where an old situation ends and something new begins.

Transition is an internal process – it's the emotional process we come to terms with the new reality.

> *"If you always do what you always did, you will always get what you always got."* – **Albert Einstein**

It's all about how we react to change.

When you feel resistance, address it immediately. Identify the root cause (the why?) and own it! If you look at every situation with a possibility mindset, that you can change the meaning you are giving it, you will create that as your reality. You don't have to have all the answers, but you can have fun looking at all the possibilities.

Here are some examples. You may want to turn your *difficulties* into *possibilities*.

Problem	Opportunity
Overwhelmed with work	Implement a time management plan
Relationship issues	Work on money blocks
Money matters	I had to give up cheese and alcohol
Management style and colleagues	Introduce coaching into my work environment

Now you have a go.

Problem	Opportunity

THE LAW OF TRANSFORMATION

"What the caterpillar calls the end of the world, the master calls a butterfly."

– **Richard Bach**

Everything that can be called life continually willingly destroys itself in order to renew itself. There are 12 steps to your journey of transformation that are inevitable; we must go through this process to succeed.

1. Unveiling – Your current reality. This is when you feel uneasy, uncomfortable or unaware of the changes that need to take place; you are lost within your story and you experience limited awareness that there is a problem or the need to change. This is where the adventure begins.

2. Awareness – Your call to change. This is when you are faced with something that makes you curious of what could be; this is the beginning of your adventure. This might be a problem or a challenge that you need to overcome. You begin to experience increased awareness of the need to change.

3. Insight – Resistant to change. This is where you are hesitant at first to embark on your journey. You will experience resistance, fear and consternation. You will refuse the potential changes in the adventure.

4. Courage – Overcoming the fear. This is where you seek guidance and work through your fears, doubts and concerns to get you ready to move forward with your new adventure or journey.

5. Inspiration – Turning back is not an option. Now is when you cross the bridge from where you are today to where you want to be. This is where you leave your old world and experience new environments, new relationships and a new way of thinking.

6. Accountability – This is where you will be tested. This is where you learn about the rules of your new world. During this time, you endure tests of strength and willpower; you will meet new friends and maybe some new foes.

7. Discovery – You may experience a setback, sometimes causing you to try a new approach or adopt new ideas. Each and every discovery will contribute to your evolution.

8. Acceptance – You may experience a major hurdle or obstacle. During this time, you may be tempted to go back to your old world. Accept, embrace and own where you are now; be empowered by all that you experience.

9. Transformation – After you learn to accept, embrace and own your hurdle, this is where you will earn the reward of accomplishing your goal. You will move through your battle and you will not give in; you are courageous, you are powerful and you will succeed. This is where you start to experience a transformation.

10. Wisdom – This is where you can return to your old environment with a new way of thinking, feeling and behaving. You feel wiser through your transformation and have this inner balance and growth about you. You have achieved a level of consciousness that will allow you to appreciate your challenges and rewards in a new light.

11. Gratitude – This is when you experience a rebirth or a reappearance of returning to your old environment, relationship or career. This is your final test where everything is at stake and you must use everything you have learned until this point.

12. Mastery – This is the most important and most powerful stage of your journey where you have gained so much knowledge and experience that you have achieved mastery as a true leader. From this point, your mission is to apply and share your knowledge to help others embark on their Journey of Transformation.

If these 12 steps created a little curiosity, brilliant! I created a 12-week online coaching program called Rise & Thrive that will guide and help you transform and reinvent your life. The program is rich in content and will create the breakthroughs required for transformation. In addition to these benefits, the online program is fun, engaging, interactive and incredibly easy to use.

Leadership and Life Coaching Online Program

https://www.riseandthrive.com.au/leadership-life-coaching/

"The big question is whether you are going to be able to say a hearty yes to your adventure" – **Joseph Campbell**

REPROGRAM YOUR MIND

"Yesterday is gone and took away its tale. Today we must live a fresh story again" – **Rumi**

Ready to unlock your potential?

You have all the tools you need now!

As always, please remember it takes 21 to 30 days to re-program the human brain. Re-programming your human brain for success produces amazing results.

You can reprogram your brain in 21 days and transform your life. Your brain is like a muscle, and like every other muscle in our bodies, your brain requires regular training and coaching in order to change. To make the shift, you can create a new mind map or simply reconfigure your existing map to remove conflict of competing values and beliefs that no longer serve you or have any purpose.

Your brain can change. Brain plasticity refers to change in neural pathways and synapses that can change your behaviour, depending on your environment. Neuroplasticity is a concept that the brain can be changed and modified through selective external interventions. The brain begins as a very simple receptor that is influenced by your environment.

Everything that exists has an energy frequency and a wavelength. Therefore, every thought that we think produces a different brainwave frequency. You can neutralise a destructive frequency into a positive frequency. Anyone who understands frequencies knows that the way to cancel a frequency is to hit it with the equal and opposite frequency. Like turning on a light in a dark room, the light always overcomes the darkness. The positive energy will overcome the negative energy.

Visualisation

'If you can imagine it and visualise it, you can create it.'

The power of visualisation is a mental technique that uses the imagination to make dreams and goals come true. Using visualisation can improve your life and attract to you success and prosperity. It is a power that can alter your environment and circumstances, cause events to happen, and attract money, possessions, work, people and love into your life.

Using visualisation will supercharge your results! Your mind doesn't know what is real and what is not real. If you can see yourself achieving your results, you are half way there.

You can't do anything that you can't picture yourself doing. Once you make the picturing process conscious and deliberate, you begin to create the self you want to be. The imagination is powerful.

How to use Visualisation

Visualisation is simple, but it requires you to practice often to get the best results out if it. Just follow the steps and enjoy the process.

Relax: Find a quiet place. Once you are settled, take a couple of deep breaths and close your eyes. Connect with your body, starting from your toes and slowly moving up to your head as you release all the tension out of your body with every breath.

Creative imagining: Depending on what you would like to visualise, you will need to create an environment for your visualisation. Let's say, you would like to be a public speaker, so you would start to imagine your setting; the venue, the stage, the décor around you, the curtains and so on. The more detail, the more real it will seem to your unconscious mind.

Dissociated: This is where you perceive yourself to be outside of you, meaning from another point of you. You are the observer of your environment. Imagine yourself coming closer to the stage where you are about to perform and continue with your painting. Use colour, add as much detail to your picture as possible. Add people to their seats, add a camera man etc.

Associated: You are now in, seeing through your own eyes and hearing the sounds of you speaking. You are feeling as if you are physically there. Feel the microphone in your hands and feel what it's like to stand up on that stage. Start practicing to speak out loud, imagine completing your speech without stopping in front of your audience just as if you were an expert. Hear them roar that they want more!

Return: Once you have tapped into all your senses and it feels real, allow yourself to slowly come back. You have completed your visualisation practice and the image slowly fades. When you feel ready, open your eyes.

The steps above work because you are strengthening the paths for that skill in your brain. Your mind doesn't even notice the difference; so, practicing this way during those times where you are away from your practice environment can truly help you improve.

Start with a simple skill that you want to learn, like waking up earlier or eating slower. That way you can practice with something easier and strengthen your visualisation skills before tackling the big ones.

Vision Board

Keep your dreams alive by creating your vision board for your goals.

A vision board is a tool used to help clarify, concentrate and maintain focus on specific life goals.

A vision board helps you:

- Identify your vision and gives it clarity
- Reinforce your daily affirmations
- Keep your attention and focus on your intentions

Firstly, decide what your vision board is going to communicate and search for images that sum that up for you. Don't forget to include a picture of yourself! Let your creativity go wild! Create with love, feeling, and all of the effort you put into your visualisations, really connect with the inspiration and motivation that you want to convey on the board. See it, hear it and feel it, as if it were now. Believe it is already yours.

How to create a vision board

Start to make notes on exactly what you want on your vision board. Try not to focus on too many things; the simpler, the better for you to create it. For example, I select 3 topics:

- Relationship
- Health
- Career

Then, with each topic, write down what your aspiration is, what you want to achieve out of each one and what your goals are. For example:

Relationship

- More time with my loved ones
- More travel
- More cooking and spending time eating

Health

- Yoga once a week
- Running twice a week
- Eating organic

Career

- Spend more time with my team (weekly)
- Write more content to share
- Travel more with my work

Once you have that all mapped out, you can choose words and images that inspire you. I like to buy an A3 red cardboard and then add all my words and pictures. One secret is that you must have a date on your board; otherwise, your goals could go on for years.

But, also be grateful for the good that is already present in your life.

Acknowledge:

- any goals that you have already achieved
- the changes you have seen and felt
- the Law of Attraction at work in your life

Look at it every night before going to bed and every morning when you wake. The more time and energy you give your vision board, the more powerful it will become. You can sit in front of your vision board and visualise every day with your visualisation techniques.

Create momentum. The smallest results create the greatest motivation!

"Sometimes it is not about trying harder, it is the little efforts every day that accumulate over time, adding up to big efforts which create change. Quantum leaps are possible in all areas of our lives, but we would not experience them as long as we stay stuck in our familiar comfort zones. A quantum leap happens when you open your mind to completely new possibilities." – **Catherine Plano**

PERSISTENCE PREVAILS

Winners never quit and quitters never win.

Persistence enables us to be sure of our success and achievement.

Don't let obstacles stand in your way. Learn from your mistakes as a way to work better. Always remember, failure is only feedback.

Develop your patience, persistence and perseverance. Defeat your procrastination through action. Success takes time and determination, so have faith, hope and believe in yourself. You will get the result you want, if you work hard enough at it.

Stay strong on your path and don't stray from your path. The power to change is in your hands – persistence means continuing firmly with a course of action despite obstacles and resistance.

Focus on the present and live in the moment. Perseverance is priceless! Knowledge comes from experience.

THE POWER OF JOURNALING

Spark your creativity!

Journaling is different from recording a diary. Journaling is to write without thinking – it's just allowing your stream of consciousness to create words on paper. Having a journal where you can write every day – how you are feeling, what are you thinking, what have you experienced and so on – will increase your creative juices. The more you do it, the more you loosen up your expression muscle.

There is a lot of research on the health benefits of journaling and some are:

- Managing anxiety
- Reducing stress
- Coping with depression
- Help you work through your fears

Journaling, like meditation, works best if it becomes a short daily habit. Of course, there are times when you feel the need to *'go deeper'*. But most of the times a paragraph will do – incorporate some doodling if you enjoy it. The purpose is to empty your head, and you'll find that afterwards you'll feel more relaxed. Those troubling or chaotic thoughts will have been dealt with, or you might have captured a gem of an idea that's been roaming around in your brain.

Insight into my journal:

Things to consider when journaling

Thoughts – *what was my thinking like today?* Review the day; take note of what was present in your mind. Replace negative thoughts into positive, empowering thoughts.

Words/Language – *what was my language like today?* Watch your words and language; replace all words that make you feel disempowered. Replace your words/language with a new empowering vocabulary.

Feelings/Emotions – *overall, how was I feeling today?* Your emotions are your indicator, your internal compass. You can replace your negative emotions with positive emotions by gradually climbing up your emotional scale. Use your power circle or pressure points to replace your negative into positive emotions.

New Habit – *how did I go with my 21-day plan?* Trick your mind into changing a habit, focus on your new habit every day for 21 days consecutively and the old one will disappear. Use your trigger or pressure point to embed the new habit.

Actions towards your goals – the more you visualise and act towards your goal, the quicker you will get to your result. Record what you did today to bring you closer to that goal.

There are so many ways that you can deep dive in and do some self-reflection and self-discovery through journaling. It can be a series of questions or as simple as how am I feeling physically, emotionally, mentally and spiritually. Or just write what comes out. It's a great insight into your psyche.

WRITE A LETTER TO YOUR FUTURE SELF

The best way to predict your future is to create it.

One of the best things you can do is write a letter to your future self. It cultivates gratitude, which is one of the best things for your emotional and mental wellbeing. Writing yourself a letter creates your future; this will assist you with sparking your creativity and excitement for it.

Give yourself permission to have fun with your letter. Think big and be grateful for what you have accomplished. The more information you add to your letter, the more it becomes a self-fulfilling prophecy.

This letter is a message in a bottle. You are to send it to yourself and you are not to open it until the date of your goal achievement. You may want to add a voucher in your letter as a little reward of your achievements.

Of course, don't forget to thank yourself for the lessons along the way. They made you who you are today and be thankful to your future self.

21-DAY ACTION PLAN TO REPROGRAM YOUR BRAIN.

Working through your 21 days – remember that you have to do it for 21 to 30 days consecutively. You can't miss one day, and if you do, you have to start all over again. This is the only way it will work.

Building a New Habit - Tracking Sheet

My NEW Habit:

My Reward:

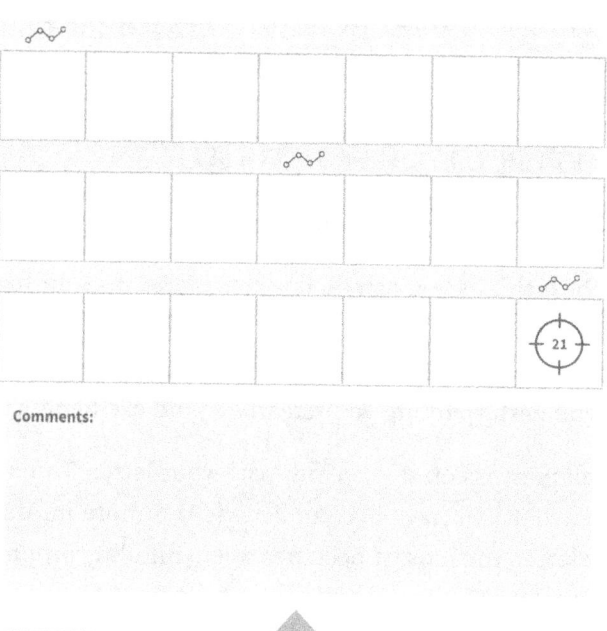

Comments:

THANK YOU

Personally, this journey has been very rewarding for me. It has taken me over a year to write this book, and in the midst of it, I found a new me. I would like to thank you for taking the time out for you and I know your journey is only the beginning now that you have all the resources and tools that you require to build a brand new you. I wish you well on your adventures.

Love and Blessings mwah x

www.ingramcontent.com/pod-product-compliance
Lightning Source LLC
Chambersburg PA
CBHW050306010526
44107CB00055B/2120